It's another Quality Book from CGP

This book is for anyone doing GCSE English.

Whatever subject you're doing it's the same old story — there are lots of facts and you've just got to learn them. KS4 English is no different.

Happily this CGP book gives you all that important information as clearly and concisely as possible.

It's also got some daft bits in to try and make the whole experience at least vaguely entertaining for you.

What CGP is all about

Our sole aim here at CGP is to produce the highest quality books — carefully written, immaculately presented and dangerously close to being funny.

Then we work our socks off to get them out to you — at the cheapest possible prices.

Contents

Section One — The Secret of Literature Essays
What Questions Really Mean 1
Example Literature Questions 2
Themes 3
Coming Up With A Theme 4
Some Themes 5
Writing Your Essay 6
Example of Planning and Writing 8
Revision Summary 10

Section Two — Looking At The Question
Reading The Instructions 11
Questions For English 12
Questions For Literature: Novels 14
Questions About Plays 16
Questions About Poems 17
Comparison Questions 18
Choosing The Right Question 19
Revision Summary 20

Section Three — Planning Your Essay
What Planning Means 21
How To Plan 22
Working Out Your Points 23
Making Your Final Plan 24
Planning English Answers 25
Story Writing 26
Planning Novel Essays 27
Planning Play Essays 28
Planning Poetry Essays 29
How To Plan Comparisons 30
Three Big Tips 32
Revision Summary 33

Section Four — Starting Your Writing
Starting An Essay 34
Your Opening Paragraph 35
Starting Other Kinds Of Answer 36
Starting Articles And Reports 37
Starting Descriptions 38
Starting Stories 39
Revision Summary 40

Section Five — Arguing Your Case
How To Argue 41
Answering The Question 42
Following Your Plan 43
Making It Clear 44
Using Clear Language 45
Linking Words 46
Two-Sided Arguments 47
Changing Your Argument 48
Four Big Tips 49
Revision Summary 50

Section Six — Quoting & Examples

Why You Need Examples 51
Quoting In Literature Essays 52
How To Quote Properly 53
Two Key Rules For Quoting 54
When To Use Speech Marks 55
Quoting From Poems & Plays 56
Other Literature Examples 57
Examples In English Essays 58
Finding English Examples 59
Revision Summary 60

Section Seven — Comparing

How To Compare 61
Comparing Two Poems 62
Writing Your Comparisons 64
Comparing Three Or Four Things 66
Common Comparison Topics 67
Revision Summary 68

Section Eight — Information Writing

Describing 69
Informing 71
Explaining 72
Revision Summary 74

Section Nine — Persuading

Persuading 75
Some Persuading Tricks 76
More On Persuading 77
Three Useful Tricks 78
Revision Summary 79

Section Ten — Ending Your Writing

Ending Your Essays 80
Problems With Essays 82
More Problems With Endings 83
Ending Letters 84
Ending Articles & Reports 85
Ending Descriptions 86
Ending Stories 87
Revision Summary 88

Section Eleven — Comprehension

Comprehension Questions 89
Media Text Comprehensions 90
Other Cultures & Traditions 95
Revision Summary 98

Index 99

Published by Coordination Group Publications Ltd.

Contributors:
Simon Cook
Taissa Csáky
James Paul Wallis

and:
Glenn Rogers
Tim Wakeling

ISBN: 978 1 84146 112 0

Groovy website: www.cgpbooks.co.uk
Jolly bits of clipart from CorelDRAW®
Printed by Elanders Hindson Ltd, Newcastle upon Tyne

Text, design, layout and illustrations © Coordination Group Publications Ltd. 1999
All rights reserved.

SECTION ONE — THE SECRET OF LITERATURE ESSAYS

What Questions Really Mean
UNDERSTANDING THE QUESTION

You can't give an answer unless you understand the question. The trouble is, they make things harder by asking tricky questions. The first secret is what the questions really mean.

The Questions Don't Say What They Mean

1) If they wrote the exams in the simplest possible way, the questions would probably be fairly easy to answer. The trouble is they don't.
2) Some questions are nice and easy. But others are written so that if you take them at face value, they seem mighty hard.
3) Learn the tricks on this page — it'll all be loads clearer.

Work Out What You're Supposed To Do

Q3: Is the play interesting?

Q11: Do you think the play is interesting?

Q7: How does the author make the play interesting?

Q2: Explain how the author makes the play interesting.

Q5: Say if you find this play interesting and why.

Q4: What makes this an interesting play?

Don't be confused by the way they ask the question. All of these are the same.

= "Talk about the interesting things in the play."

An 'interesting thing' could be a quote from the play, the language, the images, the structure, if it rhymes, the plot, the characters or the emotions.

'Why' And 'How' Really Mean 'Give Examples'

1) Loads of questions ask you to say why you think something, or how the play/novel/poem does something.
2) At first glance, there isn't much to say. Your immediate answer might be 'Because it's not boring,' or 'With a scary story.'
3) All they really want is for you to give them examples of 'things' from the play/novel/poem that have something to do with the question.

Why is this a good novel?

How is tension created?

More Than One Poem — Give Similarities And Differences

Every time the question asks you to talk about more than one poem, it wants you to compare them as part of your essay. Sometimes they tell you to compare them. Sometimes they don't. Either way, you have to talk about their similarities and differences as part of your answer.

Compare the way Keats and Frost write about nature.

How do the poets bring their memories to life in these poems?

In the exam it'd be about poems or short stories. In coursework you could have plays or novels as well.

Understanding The Question: Example Literature Questions

These questions look tricky. But if you lift the lid on what they really mean, they're loads easier.

Example Questions With What They Really Mean

What qualities make Tennyson's poems memorable?

It could say '...that make it interesting', 'good', 'powerful' or whatever. It almost always means "Say what's good about it."

= Find examples of things (images, language, emotions, 'plot') about the poem that you can say are memorable.

How is suspense created in *An Inspector Calls*? = Talk about the things that add suspense.

How have the conditions of soldiers at war been made real to you in this poem? = Talk about the things that show what it's like for the soldiers.

What attracts you to *Waiting for Thelma's Laughter* by Grace Nichols?

Say why you like this poem.

= Find examples of things (images, language, emotions, 'plot') about the poem that you can say are good or interesting.

What do you think is the most important theme in *The Importance of Being Earnest*?

= Pick out a load of themes (things the play is about), and then compare them so you can say if one of them is more important.

Do you think Mrs Bennet is a good mother in *Pride and Prejudice*?

Is Macbeth a wholly evil character?

How important are the witches in *Macbeth*?

= Find examples of Mrs Bennet/Macbeth/the witches being a good mother/wholly evil/important and talk about them. Also find examples of the opposites and talk about them.

LOOK OUT — a question about more than one poem. You have to talk about similarities and differences.

Compare these poems by Wordsworth and R. S. Thomas. Write about how the poets use language to get their ideas across.

= Talk about the two poems together, pointing out the similarities and differences. DON'T ever do half an essay on one poem, and then the second half on the other.

Literature has a dark secret — written in black ink...

Don't be bamboozled by the questions. They always want you to find examples that relate to the question, and talk about them. And if it's about more than one poem — similarities and differences.

Section One — The Secret of Literature Essays

Themes

OK, here it is. THE big secret of writing English Literature essays. This is what you need to know to write really great essays. What's more, it's dead easy once you've done a few.

You Need To Make Up A Theme

This is what makes Literature questions so hard. They don't tell you that you need a theme — and if you don't know that, it's tons harder to get the marks.

> A theme is a way of reading something clever into the bit of writing that the question's about. It's what you base your answer on — it's like a point you're trying to make.

Your theme helps you get beyond writing about exactly what the bit of writing says — but keeps it relevant.

EXAMPLES:

If the question asks you to compare two poems, your theme might be that one is much more personal than the other.

If the question asks you if Macbeth is a wholly evil character, your theme might be that he starts off as a normal person, but is corrupted to become completely evil.

You Need Examples To Back Up Your Theme

1) No one will ever agree with you if you haven't got examples (things like quotations from the writing) to back up your theme.
2) When you choose your theme, make sure there are things you can use to back it up.

Your theme can use examples from other bits of the writing, as long as your main point comes from the bit you're asked about.

EXAMPLE:

If you have a question about two poems, and your theme is that the first one is more personal than the second one, you need to be able to back it up.

You could do this by saying that the first one uses things that someone is actually saying, and talks about "you" and "I", but the second one talks about people generally.

There's Always More Than One Theme You Can Use

Often there are loads of different themes. Don't worry about getting the "right" one. As long as it's not really daft, you'll be fine.

Your theme can be totally different from everyone else's. It'll actually gain you marks, because yours will stand out from the crowd.

EXAMPLE:

If you had the Macbeth question from above, a different theme could be that Macbeth wasn't wholly evil, but in fact other people and circumstances partially controlled his actions.

SECTION ONE — THE SECRET OF LITERATURE ESSAYS

THEMES
Coming Up With a Theme

OK, so themes are great. This page helps you to think up a theme. That's the hard bit — once you've got a theme, writing the essay is easy... well, more or less.

Making Notes Helps You Think Of A Theme

Scribbling down a few notes on what the bit of writing's about makes it a lot easier to think of a theme.

Make notes about some of these — they're a good way to think up a theme.

Five Things You can Base Your Theme on
1) What happens through time — the plot of a story.
2) The language — whether it's elegant, or slang, or short and straight to the point.
3) The mood — happy, sad, angry, melancholy, ironic (be really careful if you use this one).
4) Images. The writer may have used descriptions that make pictures in your mind when you read them.
5) A hidden meaning. It may be that the poem could be about something different from what the words actually say.

When you make notes about more than one bit of writing, make the notes on them separately, then look at both sets of notes together.

EXAMPLES:

If you had a poem about someone stretching to pick the last apple from a nearly dead tree, your theme could be that the poem is really about mankind taking too much from the earth, and destroying nature. — A hidden meaning theme.

A language theme. → Your theme might be that a book is made very real to the reader because it's written the way people speak, rather than in correct English.

An image theme. → For some writing about a place, you might have a theme about how the images created make it feel as if the reader is actually there.

A mood theme. → If you're comparing two war poems, your theme could be that one is sad about people dying in war, and the other is angry about it.

No Details Are Too Small... Or Too Obvious

① It doesn't matter if you base your theme on a small detail. Even if you use one sentence to get your main idea from, that's fine.

In Shakespeare's sonnet beginning "My mistress' eyes are nothing like the sun...", there are 12 lines where he says his mistress isn't a perfect being. Then he ends with:
"...and yet, by heaven, I think my love as rare
As any she belied with false compare."
Your theme might be that although he loves her, he realises she's a human being, not a perfect goddess.
Without the last sentence, you'd think he didn't think much of her. ← So your theme has come from just one sentence.

Well my eyes are exactly like the sun.

② If you're comparing two poems and one rhymes and the other doesn't, you could write about the different effect they have because of this. It doesn't matter that it's a really obvious difference.

SECTION ONE — THE SECRET OF LITERATURE ESSAYS

Some Themes

THEMES

Thinking up a theme is _earth-shatteringly_ important — and here's some more stuff about how to do it.

You Can Make a Theme from Two Small Themes

If you can't think of a _big theme_, but it's easy to come up with a _few_ themes that don't give you enough to write about, you could put _two_ themes together to get one _bigger one_.

You might get this question:

> "How does this story make you feel like you're a part of it?"

You could write about the story being written from the _point of view_ of the _main character_ (ie using _I_ did this, _I_ said that…) _AND_ how the strong images make you feel that you're actually in the _places_ described.

"Is" Questions — You Don't have to Answer Yes or No

You might get asked something like:

> The writer compares the rebel fighters to football hooligans. Is this a good comparison?

It's best not to come down on one side or the other — show you're open minded by concluding that the statement is true to an extent.

Pick out reasons _for_ and _against_. If you've got loads of reasons _for_ then the answer would be '_yes_', if you've got loads _against_, it's '_no_'.

If you really _can't decide_ if it's a good comparison or not, don't worry. As long as you have a decent _summary_ at the end, it doesn't matter. Try something like this for your summary:

> _The comparison is accurate in some ways — for example the description of the fighting techniques, the chaos caused and the way most people there didn't want to get involved. It is not a perfect comparison, however: unlike the football hooligans, the rebel fighters have carefully planned their attacks, and work together to accomplish an aim._

Examples of Questions with Possible Themes

> Is Macbeth a wholly evil character? Give reasons for your answer.

Your theme could be:

It depends on the meaning of _wholly evil_. If it depends only on actions, he is wholly evil, but it could be argued that since he feels _guilt_, he can't be wholly evil.

There are other themes for this question on page 3.

But I'm not evil, I'm just misunderstood.

> How are you made to identify with Pip in _Great Expectations_?

Your theme could be:

The way the story starts with Pip as a _child_ makes us feel as if we have _grown up_ with him. This and the fact that the story is written as if Pip was _actually telling_ it causes us to identify with Pip.

> What makes _To Kill a Mockingbird_ a successful novel?

Your theme could be:

The feeling that the reader is actually _seeing_ the story happen is what makes this novel so successful. This is achieved by it being written as if Scout was _actually telling_ the story, and by it using realistic, informal _language_ when the characters speak.

Ith it weally about ethayth? — it themes tho...

Themes are ultra-important — they must be for me to use three pages on them. _Learn_ how to think up a theme, and make sure you _use_ them when you're answering questions — you'll get more _marks_.

SECTION ONE — THE SECRET OF LITERATURE ESSAYS

FIVE STEPS FOR WRITING ESSAYS	# Writing Your Essay

The Five Basic Steps For Writing Your Essay

OK, here's where it all comes together. Here are five steps for writing those nasty literature essays...

1. Work out what the question MEANS.
2. Make your NOTES.
3. Think of a THEME.
4. Make your PLAN.
5. WRITE your essay.

① Work Out What The Question Means

e.g. Write about how two poems from the selection describe old age. = Compare the descriptions of old age in the two poems.

Don't forget, if it mentions more than one piece of writing, then you should write about the similarites and differences.

② Make Your Notes

The point of making notes is to help you come up with a theme and plan your essay. No one else is going to look at them, so don't bother making them neat.

Note down anything you notice about the writing:
— Any unusual words or images.
— Anything you notice about the style.
— Any ideas you have about it.
— Anything else unusual.
— Any quotes or things you notice that would make good examples.
— Anything about the plot or hidden meanings.

e.g. this could be whether a poem rhymes, or whether the writer uses simple words.

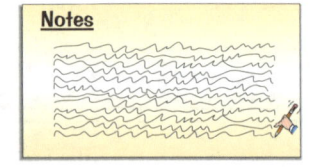

③ Think Of A Theme

You might think of a good theme when you're making your notes. If not, look through your notes and the writing again, and try thinking about these five things:

If you can think of more than one good theme, go for it. Extra themes can improve your answer. Don't have more than three or four though or your answer will sound muddled.

1. Language
2. Mood
3. Images
4. Plot
5. Hidden Meanings

If you don't have a theme, don't give up. Your answer won't be as good, but you can still write an essay.

④ Make Your Plan

The main reason for doing a plan is to work out the points you're going to make, and the order you're going to make them in.

That means a plan is basically a list of points in the right order.

It's also a good idea to note down the examples you're going to use to back up your points.

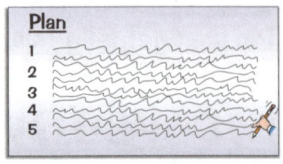

Writing Your Essay

FIVE STEPS FOR WRITING ESSAYS

⑤ Write Your Essay

OK, there are three parts to any essay — the introduction, the main bit, then the conclusion:

1. Introduction

The introduction should be one paragraph. Remember these two things:
- if it's not obvious from the title, say what your essay is about;
- say what your theme is.

2. Main Bit

This is the bit where you make all your points.
It should be much longer than the introduction and conclusion.
- Make each point in a separate paragraph.
- Back up each point with at least one example.

3. Ending

The ending should be one paragraph, and it's a summary of what you've written:
- summarise your main arguments;
- say what your theme is again.

A Few More Points

① Try to use elegant language — you'll get more marks.

② Keep it impersonal — don't use the word "I" or say things like, "in my opinion". It's much better to say things like, "The poem seems to be about..."

③ If your essay is about two bits of writing, you're always comparing them. Whenever you make a point, you should make it about both of them — it will either be a similarity or a difference. Don't just write about one piece and then the other without linking them.

④ You should always give both sides. If the question asks if a story is good, give reasons why it isn't good as well as reasons why it is.

Have a look at these bits of essay — I'll show you what I mean:

✗ *I thought the first story was great, because it described in realistic detail the feelings of the author as she was growing up. I liked the second story because of the way the writer used flashbacks to create the mood.*

This one doesn't write about both stories together. It says something about one of them, then something about the other — but it doesn't link them.

✓ *Both the stories dealt with the feelings of the author in childhood. However, the first one was written from the child's point of view, while the second was written as if someone is looking back, later in life.*

This one links the two stories together, by using words like "however" and "while". It's impersonal too — it doesn't use "I".

Essay, essay, essay — what have we 'ere then...

OK, so there's five basic steps to writing an essay: 1) work out what the question means; 2) make notes; 3) think of a theme; 4) make a plan; 5) write the essay. Make sure you know what you have to do for each step — then all you'll need is a bit of practice...

SECTION ONE — THE SECRET OF LITERATURE ESSAYS

Example of Planning and Writing

EXAMPLE PLAN & ESSAY

The only way to get it <u>clear</u> how the Five Essay Writing Steps work <u>in action</u>, is to go through this <u>example</u>. Have a <u>really</u> good look at how I've followed the <u>steps</u> to come up with a great essay.

① Work Out *What* The Question *Means*

Q3. What features make "Composed Upon Westminster Bridge" a *successful* poem?

You may wish to consider:

- Wordsworth's style of writing
- the ideas in the poem
- Wordsworth's use of words and images

as well as any ideas of your own.

These are things you've <u>definitely</u> got to look at in your answer.

You <u>can</u> write about anything <u>you think</u> goes with the question.

= Find examples of things (images, language, emotions, 'plot') about the poem that you can say are <u>good</u>.

Composed Upon Westminster Bridge
Sept. 3, 1802

Earth has not anything to show more fair:
Dull would he be of soul who could pass by
A sight so touching in its majesty;
This City now doth, like a garment, wear
The beauty of the morning; silent, bare,
Ships, towers, domes, theatres, and temples lie
Open unto the fields, and to the sky;
All bright and glittering in the smokeless air.
Never did sun more beautifully steep
In his first splendour, valley, rock or hill;
Ne'er saw I, never felt, a calm so deep!
The river glideth at his own sweet will:
Dear God! the very houses seem asleep;
And all that mighty heart is lying still!
(William Wordsworth)

② Make Your *Notes*

Go through the poem and note down <u>anything</u> you notice.

NOTES

* The poem is about morning on Westminster Bridge, and how beautiful the city looks — "Earth has not anything to show more fair."
* It celebrates the "majesty" of the sight, saying anyone who passed it by would be "Dull" of soul.
* Lines 4-8 give a long description of what he sees. He uses an image of "the beauty of the morning" being like a "garment" which the city is wearing, as if the city is a person — and describes all the features he can see "Ships, towers etc." lying "silent" and "bare" to the fields and the sky. The whole city is in view "All bright and glittering in the smokeless air", so he can see its beauty.
* In line 9 the poem changes — it talks about the beauty of the sight he's just described, and says the rising of the sun (its "first splendour") looks just as beautiful <u>here</u> as it does over any "valley", "rock" or "hill".
* He says how calm the city is. Then he describes the river as having human characteristics — travelling at "his own sweet will" — and the houses too, because they "seem asleep". He sounds surprised at how quiet everything is — he says that the "mighty heart" of the city is "lying still!"
* The poem is a sonnet — it has fourteen lines. Sonnets are usually a kind of love poem — so perhaps this is a <u>love poem about the city</u>.

Some notes don't get used in the final essay, but you need to make notes on <u>everything</u> so you know what's going on.

This is about the <u>words</u> and <u>images</u> in the poem.

Look for useful <u>examples</u>.

These are unusual <u>images</u>.

This is about the <u>structure</u> of the essay. It's kind of about <u>hidden meanings</u> too. Anything clever like this will make a really good point for your essay.

SECTION ONE — THE SECRET OF LITERATURE ESSAYS

Example of Planning and Writing

EXAMPLE PLAN & ESSAY

③ Think Of A Theme

First of all, we've already got two themes:
1) It's a love poem about the city.
2) He describes things like they're people.

There's plenty more themes you could come up with — don't forget to look at the <u>language</u>, <u>mood</u>, <u>images</u>, <u>plot</u> and any <u>hidden meanings</u>.

> *It's a successful poem because it describes a place that many people know, but it describes it in a new and eye-opening way.*

> *The poem describes how peaceful the city is, but hints that it isn't so beautiful when the "mighty heart" wakes up.*

> *The poem celebrates the power of nature and mocks man's self-importance. The city appears fragile — it is "open to the fields and to the sky". To the sun it appears no different from any other part of nature (any "valley, rock or hill"). The river glides at its "own sweet will", taking no notice of our actions.*

④ Make Your Plan

PLAN
1) It's a love poem about the city. Wordsworth describes the city as if it were a person, wearing the "beauty of the morning".
2) The poem is full of images of "beauty" and of nature. Wordsworth gives a long description of his view across the city in lines 4-8, and then compares it to other sunrises in nature.
3) He describes things as having human characteristics: the river travels at "his own sweet will", the houses "seem asleep" and the "mighty heart" of the city is "lying still"...

These are the <u>points</u> you're going to make, in the right <u>order</u>.

Note down <u>quotes</u> and <u>examples</u> that you're going to use, so you don't forget.

⑤ Write Your Essay

Make it totally clear which <u>question</u> you're answering.

Say <u>what</u> the essay's about <u>straight away</u>.

Question 3.

"Composed Upon Westminster Bridge" is a successful poem because it describes the dawn over Westminster in beautiful language, as if Wordsworth is writing a love poem to the city. The poem is a sonnet, which is often a kind of love poem. Most of all though, the language and images of the poem make it sound like a love poem.

At several points in the poem, Wordsworth describes the city as if it is a person. He talks about it wearing the "beauty of the morning" like a "garment", as if he is looking at someone wearing a beautiful dress.

At the end of the poem, he talks about the stillness and calm of the city: "And all that mighty heart is lying still!" The city doesn't really have a heart. Wordsworth is exaggerating, using a special poetic language to bring his description of the dawn to life...

This is all <u>impersonal</u>. There are no "I think" bits in here.

Each point's in a <u>separate paragraph</u>.

Use good <u>examples</u> to back up each point.

Remember to use <u>elegant language</u> — 'stillness', 'exaggerating', 'poetic'.

(THERE'D BE MORE MAIN BIT, BUT I'LL JUMP STRAIGHT TO THE ENDING.)

To Wordsworth, there is nothing more beautiful, "more fair", than the city in the morning. His description captures the moment of calm before the day begins. He makes it clear to us that this is when he loves Westminster most. The poem is successful exactly because it shows us his feelings so vividly, and makes us want to share them as well.

The ending is a good <u>summary</u> of what you've said in the essay.

The last sentence links it back to the <u>question</u> — why the poem's '<u>successful</u>'.

SECTION ONE — THE SECRET OF LITERATURE ESSAYS

REVISION SUMMARY

Revision Summary

Phew, it's pretty heavy going. And that's only nine pages. But the thing is, it'll get you higher marks in the exam. If you get to grips with the stuff in this section, then the whole of the book will be easier. The way to make sure you've learnt this stuff is to check you can do all of these questions. Try them all, and look up any you can't do. Then try them all again. Keep doing that until you can answer all of them. THEN you really know this stuff.

1) What two things do you need to talk about when the question asks about more than one poem?

2) If the question asks why you like a poem/play/novel, what kind of things could you talk about?

3) Here's a question: "Do you think Ralph is a good leader in *Lord of the Flies?*"
Spud Boy reckons you should just look for things that show he's a good leader.
Pea Head says you should only look for things that show he's bad.
Are either of them right? If not, what should you do?

4) How do you back up your theme so people will believe it?

5) Can you base your theme on a really small part of the writing?

6) Can you use examples from other parts of the writing?

7) When you're making notes to help you come up with a theme, what five things do you need to think about?

8) What can you do if you can think of a few themes, but none of them will give you enough to write about?

9) What should you do if you're asked "Is blurg good?", and you can't decide whether it's good or not?

10) What are the five basic steps for writing a literature essay?

11) Is it okay to have more than one theme for your essay?

12) What two things do you need to remember about the introduction to your essay?

13) In the main bit of your essay, what two things should you do every time you make a point?

14) What two things do you need to remember when writing the ending to your essay?

15) You should keep your essay 'impersonal'. What does that mean?

But that's 'Litter-ature'...

SECTION ONE — THE SECRET OF LITERATURE ESSAYS

SECTION TWO — LOOKING AT THE QUESTION

Reading the Instructions
READING THE EXAM PAPER THROUGH

If there's one bit of advice that'll make any difference to your GCSE results, it's this: read every question properly, and work out exactly what it's you're supposed to do.

Start By Reading The Instructions On The Paper

This looks so stupid it hardly seems worth doing. That's completely wrong though. In exams or coursework it's really easy to forget the simple things and rush into the questions without thinking. That's the quick route to blowing it — and don't think I'm joking.

> Answer one question from Section A and one question from Section B.

There's no way around it — you must follow any instructions like this.

> Spend about one hour on this Section.

I always follow instructions...

This is a helpful tip from an exam paper. It's there to make sure you don't waste all your time on one part of the paper and forget the rest.

The Question Paper Will Tell You To Do Some Things

1) Two simple little things to do here. If you don't do them both, you'll definitely lose marks.

> Make sure you plan your answer and write in paragraphs.

2) Look at this. All it's asking you to do is write more than 300 and less than 400 words. Talk about easy marks — just don't write any more or less.

> You should write between 300-400 words.

1000's about 200, innit?

Not too much!

3) This is a tad more difficult, because of that sneaky word "about".

> Write a report of about 200 words.

4) It really means no less than 200, but no more than 210. You're being marked on how well you fit a report into 200 words.

Remember — you'll get more marks by reading the instructions and doing what they say. Now that's an easy way to improve your grade.

Like ringing a bell — doing as you're tolled...

It's very simple really, so learn it now. If the question paper tells you to do something, you've got to do it, end of story. If you don't, then you're throwing marks away, and you can't afford to do that.

Questions For English

GCSE ENGLISH QUESTIONS

It doesn't matter if it's for coursework or the exam — you have to read the question carefully. The main thing with GCSE English questions is working out what they're testing you on.

English Questions Can Be About Opinions

1) Here's a typical question. They give you an opinion about a tricky topic, then ask you to write for or against it.

> Statement: "Young people should not be allowed to take part in dangerous sports." Write an article of about 200 words for your school newspaper in which you argue either for or against the statement.

2) You need to give your own opinion, and make sure you answer the question.

3) The good news is the question paper gives you some handy hints for your answer.

> If you are arguing for, include — injury, risks, cost.
> If you are arguing against, include — enjoyment, achievement, choice.

4) Whichever side you choose, you must put these hints in as part of your argument. They're there to help you make a plan, and to give you an idea of what the examiners want you to write.

> Remember: your purpose is to write an argument;
> to keep your audience in mind;
> to write accurately and express yourself clearly. (16 marks)

5) You even get some final tips to remind you exactly what you're doing — writing an argument — and telling you to think about what a school newspaper article is like.

Warning — Some Questions Seem Easier Than They Are

Watch out — this looks really easy.

> Describe one of the following in such a way that it can be easily imagined by your reader:
> - a city at night
> - a deserted beach
> - a busy shopping centre.

It doesn't give you many clues though, so it'll be a lot harder to think of things to write about.

Typical English questions — "more tea vicar?"...

There's only one way to prepare yourself for your English exams — practice. Get into the habit of doing exactly what the question tells you. Start by following all the instructions and using the tips in the question to help you. Always check how many marks you get for each question too.

SECTION TWO — LOOKING AT THE QUESTION

More English Questions

SITUATION & READING QUESTIONS

Reading through question papers is a real pain — but if you don't, you could have big problems. The best chance you have of getting a decent mark is by learning the golden rule.

The Golden Rule:

> When you have a choice of different questions, make sure you read them all before you start. Don't jump straight in and pick the ones that seem easy.

Some Questions Put You In A Real-life Situation

Here's the situation... *...and here's the question.*

You have a part time job. You arrive late and are sacked. You feel you were not given the chance to explain. Write a letter of about 200 words in which you try to persuade your employer to give you back your job.

Remember: you are writing a letter
the purpose of your writing
to write accurately and express yourself clearly.

I'm gonna be late!

You've got to follow these tips in order to answer the question.

A group of friends is organising an event to raise money for refugees. Prepare detailed instructions on how best to do this. You should include:
- the sort of event that will work well
- how to plan the event
- what targets to set
- how to avoid problems
- how to look after the money.

The pig show-jumping was a real money spinner.

This question wants you to do lots of things. You must include all the information you're told to, otherwise you won't get all the marks.

You Can Have Questions About Your Reading Too

Some English questions ask you to write about books, poems or articles you've read.

Choose two of Wordsworth's poems that you think have something important to say.
Explain: - what the important ideas are in each poem
- how Wordsworth brings these ideas out.

You need to explain what each poem is about and how they've been written to show these things.

Being caught by a fish hook — a reel-life situation...

Different questions want different things. Don't rush to start writing — read them all first.

SECTION TWO — LOOKING AT THE QUESTION

GCSE English Lit. Questions

Questions For Literature: Novels

These questions are about the novels, plays and poems you've read during your course.

Follow These Two Rules For Literature Questions

① Remember the Golden Rule (p.13) — read all the questions through before you decide which ones to answer.

② Make sure you know the book well so that you can answer the question.

Some Questions Are About One Character In A Novel

This sort of question is really common — and quite easy too. It gives you an opinion about a character — you've got to give reasons for and against the opinion.

> Do you think Mrs Bennet is a good mother in Pride and Prejudice?
> You may wish to consider:
> - her wish to find husbands for her daughters
> - her unpopularity with other characters in the novel
> - her reaction to Elizabeth's rejection of Collins
> - her views on Lydia's elopement.

Use this list of clues they give you to find examples for your essay.

Here's another kind of question. It's asking you how a character has changed during the book.

> How is Ralph changed by his experiences on the island in Lord of the Flies?
> You should consider:
> - what he is like when the boys are first stranded on the island
> - what he tries to do and how he responds to events and other characters
> - how the writer tries to show us the character of Ralph
> - what you think the writer wants Ralph to represent.

Watch out though — the last two points in the list are asking you about the writer. Don't leave that part out when you answer the question.

You need to think about Ralph before, during and after to answer this one.

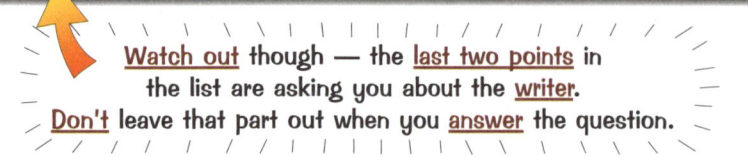

What's new in this book — a novel question...

Phew. If this lot looks really off-putting, then break the page down and go over it bit by bit. Start by learning the two rules for literature questions. Always answer all the parts of a question.

Section Two — Looking At The Question

More Novel Questions

EVENT, THEME & STYLE QUESTIONS

Questions about novels can get incredibly long and difficult. The only way to make sure you're answering them properly is to work out exactly what each bit of the question wants you to do.

Some Questions Ask For More Than One Thing

> Write about the relationship between George and Lennie in *Of Mice and Men*. What is it that holds them together, and why does George decide to kill Lennie?

1) This is about the relationship during the book.

2) But this is about what changes in the relationship at the end. The question is about two things, not just one.

3) Look at the first two helpful tips. They're both about George and Lennie's relationship during the book. They're here to help you answer the first part of the question.

> You should consider:
> - their hopes, fears and dreams
> - the kind of relationship they have, and what it gives to each of them
> - how the writer brings out the differences between them
> - why the writer chooses to end the novel with George killing Lennie.

4) These second two tips are about how the book shows the differences between George and Lennie, and why the writer decided George should kill Lennie. Use them to answer the second part of the question.

Some Are About Things That Happen In The Novel

This question would come together with the bit from Wuthering Heights that it asks about.

> Heathcliff overhears part of this conversation between Nelly Dean and Catherine Earnshaw. What effect does this have on future events in the novel?

I couldn't help it!

You're being asked to explain how this bit fits into the rest of the book.

A Few Questions Ask About the Style Of The Novel

> What qualities make *The Mayor of Casterbridge* a good novel?
> You should consider:
> - plot and variety of characters
> - Hardy's use of setting and atmosphere
> - Hardy's style of writing, including his descriptions of people and events.

We're 'head-gehogs', geddit?
Pat's new hairstyle was attracting the hedgehogs.

This difficult-sounding question is asking you to write about which of these things makes the book good — you'll have to give examples from the book to show what you mean.

SECTION TWO — LOOKING AT THE QUESTION

CHARACTER, STYLE & OPINIONS

Questions About Plays

Here's some great news. The questions you'll get asked about plays are very similar to the ones we've already looked at for novels.

You'll Definitely Get Questions About Characters

This is a question about a character. It's also about one specific thing he does in the play.

> Does John Proctor make the right decision at the end of *The Crucible*? Give reasons for your answer. You may wish to consider:
> - the events leading up to the final scene
> - Proctor's words and actions and their consequences
> - Proctor's relationships with Abigail and Elizabeth.

Ta daa! 'Carrot ears'...

You have to give an opinion here about whether John Proctor's decision is right. The best way to do that is to give the reasons for and against, and then make your decision.

Some Questions Ask About The Style And Effect

Here's a cunning little question about the style of the play — what it's like — and the effect it has on the audience.

Didn't they say 'Insect Snorkels'?

> How is suspense created in *An Inspector Calls*? You may wish to consider:
> - the atmosphere and mood
> - the inspector's appearance and manner
> - the reactions of those questioned.

Don't forget — plays are written to be performed in front of an audience, so all the important bits have to be in the characters' speeches and how they look and act on stage.

Be Careful With Questions That Ask Your Opinion

> What do you think is the most important theme in *The Importance of Being Earnest*? You may wish to consider:
> - the difference between what the characters do and what they say
> - the relationships between the male characters and the female characters
> - the social and historical background to the play.

These questions can be incredibly nasty. Don't just jump in and give your opinion straightaway. Instead, you need to talk aabout lots of different themes in the play before you decide on the most important one.

I like trapdoors in plays — it's a stage I'm going through...

Look at all three of these questions very carefully. You must learn to spot what questions like these are asking you to do. After all, you've got to answer each question properly to pick up the marks.

SECTION TWO — LOOKING AT THE QUESTION

Questions About Poems

SINGLE POEM & AUTHOR QUESTIONS

The best thing about essays on poems is they always ask the same kinds of question.

There Are Always Questions About Single Poems

There are loads of questions like this about poems. This is the key word for your answer.

> What qualities make "The Lady of Shalott" a **memorable** poem?
> You may wish to consider:
> - Tennyson's descriptions of Lancelot and the Lady
> - his skills as a storyteller, using setting and atmosphere
> - the poem's structure and style.

Your answer has got to be about what makes the poem memorable — the things about it that stick in your head — and you must include all the things in the list of clues.

You'll get questions like this with different key words, like 'good', 'powerful' or 'thought-provoking'.

You'll Be Asked About Several Poems By One Author

Another big favourite. It's asking you to write about why you find at least two of the author's poems interesting. To do this, you need to write about the things that the poems have in common, and how they're different.

> What aspects of Christina Rossetti's poetry capture your interest?
> Refer closely to two or more poems in your answer.
> You may wish to consider:
> - Rossetti's use of words and images
> - her descriptions of characters, places or events
> - her use of rhyme and rhythm.

Don't panic though — this list of clues tells you exactly which things to look for in the different poems.

The secret here is to show you've read the poems and can spot the similarities and differences — use the list of clues.

The Ancient Mariner — verse things happen at sea...

This poetry lark can seem pretty easy — but that's where you can land yourself in serious trouble. Poems are a lot shorter than novels or plays — you have to look at them much more closely to find things to write about. You need to make sure you know the poems you're writing about really well. If you don't, then you're in danger of getting very bad marks for that essay.

SECTION TWO — LOOKING AT THE QUESTION

Questions On Comparing Texts

Comparison Questions

These are some of the hardest questions. They ask you to compare poems by different authors. Remember — comparing means talking about the similarities and the differences between things.

Comparing How Two Poets Write About Something

1) The question asks you about Hopkins and Eliot.   2) You need to compare how they create a sense of place.

> Compare the ways Hopkins and Eliot create a strong sense of place in their poems. Choose at least one poem by each poet and write about:
> - what sort of place is being described
> - what the poets feel about these places
> - how they describe the place and how their choice of words brings out their feelings
> - your own response to the poems you have chosen.

3) The list tells you what to look for in each individual poem. You've got to compare the different answers you get from the poems you're talking about.

Be Careful Comparing More Than Two Poems

This is where it gets really tough. The question tells you what the poems show — how different love can be.

> Write about three or four poems from this group which show how different love can be. You may wish to consider:
> - the happiness and pain of love
> - the humorous side of love
> - ideal and real romance
> - differences in the ways the poems are written.

You need to give examples from the poems to highlight the different kinds of love that they show.

Here's a question about the language used in several different poems.

> Choose three or four poems from this group. What differences in the use of language do you notice? You should write about:
> - language which tells you about background and character
> - language which is formal and informal
> - words which are chosen for a particular effect.

You've got to look for examples of these things in the poems to show the differences between them.

Good comedy hosts — they're beyond compére...

Comparison questions are always tricky. You need to make sure you find plenty of examples in all of the poems — and work out the similarities and differences between them. It's the only way.

SECTION TWO — LOOKING AT THE QUESTION

Choosing The Right Question

WHICH QUESTION TO ANSWER

This whole section has been about the kinds of question you'll come across in your GCSEs. That's not all, though. It's also about helping you pick the right questions to answer.

Picking The Right Question Can Help Your Marks

1) It's simple really. Some questions are harder than others. You need to pick the questions that you can answer.

2) You've got to find the questions you know something about. Don't rush into a question if you haven't got a clue about it.

Picking your nose doesn't help.

Always Read Every Question On The Paper

Believe me, it isn't a waste of time. You have to make sure you don't miss any easy questions. If you jump into the first question you come across, you'll have no chance of a decent mark. THINK before you decide.

Narrow Your Choices Down

1) You only need to read the paper through quickly.
2) As you go, put a pencil mark beside any question you think you can answer.
3) Then work out exactly what these questions are asking you to do.
4) Finally, pick the ones you're going to answer.

> Make sure you know how many questions you're meant to answer. On some papers, you answer one question from each section.

Your Answer Must Match The Question

1) If you learn one thing from this section, learn this: unless you do what the question wants you to do, you'll lose marks.

2) Start by working out what the question really means, like we've been doing in this section.

3) If you really don't understand part of a question, don't try to answer it.

Answer the question, or else!
Ants are what?

Always read the paper — except in the loo...

Phew. Seems like a big fuss over a few questions — but it's worth it. Make sure you go over this section again, until you know how to spot exactly what a question is asking. That's the real skill.

SECTION TWO — LOOKING AT THE QUESTION

Revision Summary

Weird. A whole section on questions... but there's NOTHING worse than not reading the question and not sticking to the point in your answer. The best way to make sure you know all about it is to go through the things on this page over and over again, until it's as easy as falling off a slippy log. Remember — the secret of revision is finding out what you don't know, and then learning it till you do.

1) When should you read the instructions on the exam paper?
2) What kind of things can go wrong if you don't bother reading the instructions?
3) If it says 'write about 200 words' in an exam paper, how much can you write?
4) What types of questions do you get for English (not English Literature)?
5) Should you bother doing what the question says about handy hints and 'remember' bits?
6) What's the golden rule about when there's a choice of questions and reading them?
7) My mate Gunzo reckons he can answer English Literature questions without knowing the book well. Is he a) right b) totally wrong and in deep deep trouble?
8) Give two different kinds of question that can be asked about a character in a novel.
9) What three main kinds of question do they ask about plays?
10) For questions on the effect of plays, is it important to think how the play would be performed?
11) What sort of questions do you get asked about single poems?
12) What kind of questions do they ask about several poems by the same author?
13) With these kind of questions (see Q12) what sort of similarities should you look out for?
14) Poems are shorter than novels, so you need to look at them
    a) not a bit closer b) 5cm closer c) loads closer?
15) What are the different kinds of question about more than one poem you can be asked?
16) Why is picking the right question important?
17) Why should you read every question on the paper?
18) How do you narrow down your choices?
19) What's the important thing to remember about the number of questions you have to do?
20) What should you do if you don't know much about the topic of a question?
21) What do you need to work out about each question you've chosen?
22) If you really don't understand part of a question, should you spend time making up an answer?
23) So, all in all, how important is it to read the questions really really thoroughly? (Try 'very'.)

Some questions need to be looked at harder than others.

SECTION TWO — *LOOKING AT THE QUESTION*

SECTION THREE — PLANNING YOUR ESSAY

What Planning Means

Planning your work is incredibly boring, but there's no way you'll get the marks you need without it. You really must plan your answers before you start writing. Otherwise they'll just end up a mess.

You Must Think Before You Start Your Answer

This is what planning is all about. Once you've looked at the question and worked out what it wants you to do, you need to work out how you're going to answer it.

Your Plan = Your Ideas For Your Answer

1) Your plan is what you're going to put in your answer.
2) It's your opinions and ideas and the points you want to make.

This Is What Planning Means — Learn It Now

> Planning your essay means coming up with ideas for your answer, and working out what order you're going to put them in.

Use The Question Points For Your Plan

Here's the main question. You've got to write your essay in a certain style.

> Write an article for a teenage magazine in which you **argue** the case for more help to be given to the homeless. You should:
> - outline the present situation
> - give examples of the sort of people affected by homelessness
> - suggest what more can be done

You need to answer each of these points if you want to get good marks.

The easy way to make sure you answer each point is to use them as parts of your plan.

Scribble some quick notes for your answers.

> Helping the Homeless — teenage magazine.
> – the present situation: lots of homeless; not enough shelters.
> – examples of homeless: runaways from home; ex-soldiers etc.
> – what can be done? more shelters; education & housing schemes.

Plan it — make your writing out of this world...

If there's one thing that'll help you get a better grade in your exams, then this is it: plan your essay before you start to write. Planning means deciding what you want to say. If you just write down a jumble of different ideas in any old order, there's no way that your essay will be any good at all.

How To Plan

How To Start Your Planning

Planning is a <u>difficult</u> business, because you're itching to <u>start writing</u> your answer immediately. That's where most people go <u>wrong</u>. They <u>don't</u> plan properly, and they <u>rush</u> into their writing.

Planning Will Actually Save You Time Later

The Three Benefits Of Planning

1) Your essay will <u>stick to the point</u> better. If you don't plan, your writing will wander and you won't answer the question properly.
2) You won't suddenly run out of things to write. <u>Never</u> rush into your writing <u>without</u> stopping and thinking first.
3) Planning helps you <u>sort</u> your ideas out and put them in a <u>clear order</u>. It'll help you write a <u>clear</u> essay.

Ah, the wise one plans, ah.

Example Question — Write Notes First

1) You must <u>look carefully</u> at what the question is <u>asking</u>.

> What does Chaucer have to tell you about the character of the Prioress in the General Prologue to *The Canterbury Tales*?

WATCH OUT — this is a <u>tough</u> example. Don't worry if you <u>don't know</u> the book. Just <u>learn</u> the <u>method</u> for planning.

2) You need to start by <u>writing out</u> the title. You <u>don't</u> have to write it in full — <u>notes</u> will do.

> *What's Ch. telling you about Prior.'s charact. in Gen. Prol.?*

3) <u>Read</u> the bit about the Prioress in the General Prologue. Make <u>rough notes</u> of <u>anything</u> you think is <u>important</u>.

> *v. simple and coy - she swears "by Seinte Loy" - why?*
> *good singer/speaks french and eats v. politely- v. stately*
> *charitable - weeps if mouse hurt BUT feeds dogs expens. meat*

4) <u>Don't worry</u> about what <u>order</u> you put these notes in yet. <u>Go through</u> your notes and think about <u>how</u> you can <u>use</u> them to <u>answer</u> the question.

5) You need to <u>work out</u> what Chaucer really <u>means</u> when he tells you things about the Prioress. Write your notes out again, dividing them into the <u>opinions</u> Chaucer gives about her, and the <u>evidence</u> he uses to back them up.

Opinions:	*Evidence for or against / Comments:*
smiling simple & coy	no evidence for this
sings service well	intoned in her nose
speaks French 'ful faire'	but NOT real French - pretend French from Stratford
good table manners	wipes her lips and doesn't drop food - v. posh
stately, dignified	takes pains to pretend to be cheerful ('countrefete')
charitable, 'pitous'	weeps if sees mouse in a trap; feeds her dogs roast meat

6) Straightaway you should <u>spot</u> that some of the opinions <u>don't fit</u> with the evidence — she speaks French well, but it <u>isn't</u> real French; she's charitable, but <u>only</u> to animals.

SECTION THREE — PLANNING YOUR ESSAY

Working Out Your Points

WORKING OUT YOUR THEME

This is the really tricky bit of planning — turning your notes into a list of points that answer the question. It's all about working out what the evidence means.

Example Question — Look At Your Notes To Find A Theme

Now you know that Chaucer's evidence and opinions don't match, you need to ask one question: why does he tell you one thing and then tell you something different or opposite?

1) You need to take each opinion in your list and look at it on its own — don't worry, you don't have to write it out.

> Ch. says she's "so charitable" that she cries when a mouse is trapped.

I've heard of charity, but this is ridiculous!

2) You've got to ask yourself what Chaucer means when he says that.

> The Prioress is a nun, so she should be involved with charity, like Mother Teresa. Chaucer says she's "so charitable" that she cares about animals. He doesn't say anything about charity to people. That means when he says she's "so charitable", he's making a joke. She isn't at all. Ch. is actually criticising her.

3) Here's your first point. Next you need to find another one. Look at the notes again.

> Ch. says she speaks French "ful faire and fetisly" (elegantly) after the school of Stratford at Bowe — French of Paris was unknown to her.

4) Now you have to think about what Chaucer really means.

DON'T PANIC — you don't need to write all this stuff out. It's only here to show you how to find the right bits.

> Ch. says she speaks French well, but only pretend French. She doesn't know real French — so her French is useless, except for showing off. Ch. says she speaks it "ful faire" as a joke — he's criticising her again for pretending to be something she isn't.

5) Here's your second point — and it's very similar to your first one. You need to keep on working through until you've got a list of five or six points.

6) Then you've got to decide on the main point for your answer.

We're not what we seem.
Try telling that to her!

> Ch. keeps criticising the Prioress. Whenever he seems to say something good about her, it isn't really good at all. In other words, the main thing he's telling us is that she isn't what she seems.

7) Phew — at last. This is your main point. It's a clear answer to the question, so that's where you need to start your essay.

Like changing rail line — you need lots of points...

Plenty of things to learn. You won't just find answers in the writing — you need to work them out.

SECTION THREE — PLANNING YOUR ESSAY

Writing Your Plan

DRAWING UP YOUR PLAN

Once you've worked out your main point, you need to put all your points into a plan.
Put them in a clear order so that they give a good answer to the question.

Start Your Plan With Your Main Point

1) You must start with your main point.

   Main point first.

   > Ch. tells us Pr. isn't what she seems

2) Then move on to your next point — you need to give an example to back up your main point.

   > — tries hard to be posh but isn't - polite table manners, speaks pretend French which is useless

3) You have to give evidence for each point you make, and explain why it backs up your answer.

   > — she hides her feelings and acts dignified - but she's supposed to be a nun, who should be humble

4) You don't need to write full sentences — just notes to help you remember what you're going to write.

   I've been writing notes...

   > — she is charitable towards animals - no one else: spends money on feeding dogs roast meat, & she is only tender-hearted if the dogs are badly treated
   > — dresses v. elegant, with jewels etc - not like a nun

5) If you suddenly have a brainwave about one of your points, or about something else, stick it in your plan as well.

This List Of Points Is The Plan For Your Essay

This is the plan you've got to use for your writing.
Don't start your final plan until you've worked out all your points. And remember these four things:

1) Make sure your plan fits the question.
2) Don't be afraid to add new ideas when you're writing.
3) Your plan is there to help you — don't worry if you have to change it while you're writing.
4) You're being marked on your writing, not your plan. If the plan isn't helping, don't stick to it blindly.

Hmf?! *I'll help you mate!*

Learn this lot and it'll be plan sailing...

Plans aren't as scary as they sound. Planning just means taking your main point and then writing your other points down in order. That's the order you've got to put them in when you start writing the real thing. Your plan's there to help you — you can always change it if you need to.

SECTION THREE — PLANNING YOUR ESSAY

Planning English Answers

How To Plan English Answers

This page is all about how to plan the different kinds of writing you'll need for your essays. English answers follow the pattern we've looked at, but usually without books to help.

You Must Plan A Case To Argue For This Question

Here's a clear statement.

> "Young people should not be allowed to take part in dangerous sporting activities."

And here's the question that goes with it.

> Write an article of about 200 words for your school newspaper in which you argue either for or against this statement.
> If you are arguing for it, you should include injury, risks and cost.
> If you are arguing against it, you should include enjoyment, achievement and free choice.

You need to use these bits to help you plan your answer.

With Some Questions You Have To Support A Side

Here the question tells you to make up your mind for or against the statement.

Then you've got to make a list of points for your plan.

Don't forget to use the helpful bits from the question.

> AGAINST:
> 1. young people enjoy dangerous sports - they get a buzz - e.g. bungee jumping
> 2. they feel they've achieved something - white water rafting - they've tested themselves and they've conquered their fears.
> 3. people should be allowed to choose if they're old enough - it's their life
> 4. young people are fitter, so they have the chance to do these things - maybe when they're older, they won't.

You've only got 200 words for your answer, so you need to make your points as quickly and clearly as possible. Put them in the same order as the question.

Holiday packing — that's planning a case...

Planning English work means looking at the kind of question carefully. It could be a letter, a report or an article — you've got to plan them all the same way, using the helpful bits from the question.

SECTION THREE — PLANNING YOUR ESSAY

| How To Plan Stories | # Story Writing |

A lot of English papers have <u>one question</u> that asks you to write about something that <u>happened</u> to <u>you</u>. Watch out for this — <u>planning</u> stories is incredibly <u>tricky</u>.

Planning A Story Is As Difficult As Planning An Essay

<u>Don't</u> start thinking that stories are easy.
Unless you plan them <u>carefully</u>, you can <u>lose</u> loads of marks.

> Write about a time when you were afraid.

First You Need To Think Of Something To Write About

1) Think about any real <u>experiences</u> you've had that <u>fit</u> with the question, and scribble them down.

> — Lost in supermarket = possible but boring
> — Stuck on mountain when Steve broke his leg climbing - add some extra details

2) You've got to <u>work out</u> exactly what <u>happens</u> in the story <u>before</u> you start writing. Scribble down <u>who's</u> in it, <u>what</u> happens and <u>what feelings</u> you're going to describe.

> = about being <u>afraid</u>: me, Steve, Pete & Joe trapped on mountain; bad weather; no one else about; had some food, but not enough warm clothes - cold & hungry - worried Steve in pain - first aid (others went for help)

Who forgot the warm clothes?

3) You <u>also</u> need to plan how you're going to <u>start</u> the story and how you're going to <u>end</u> it.

> START: trapped in the forest: night falling; rustling in the bushes - cold - <u>I was scared</u>

4) You need to make it <u>exciting</u> and <u>dramatic</u> to read — start in the <u>middle</u> of the action, and write about <u>being afraid</u> straightaway.

Don't Plan A Long Piece — Keep It Simple

You <u>haven't</u> got time to write a novel — keep your plan <u>short</u>.
Make sure it's <u>relevant</u> to the question, and try to <u>bring it to life</u> when you start writing.

Dickens was a liar — he kept telling tales...

Story writing can be a hassle. Sometimes you <u>can't</u> think of anything <u>relevant</u> or <u>interesting</u> to write about. <u>Don't</u> worry — keep your writing <u>clear</u> and write about your <u>feelings</u>, and you'll be fine.

de
Planning Novel Essays

How To Plan A Novel Essay

Literature essays are easier to plan — all you have to do is remember to use the points of the question to help you. Be careful with novels though — you need to write about the whole book.

Don't Forget The Question Points To Help You Plan

You need to give a clear answer to this question.

> Who do you blame for Henchard's downfall?
> Give reasons for your answer.
> You may wish to consider:
> - the important events in Henchard's life
> - his change of fortune and the role of Fate
> - his behaviour towards other people.

Don't forget — each of these points should be part of your plan.

Your Plan Needs To Cover The Whole Book

The secret of planning novel essays is finding details from the whole book to back up your answer.

I'm covering the whole book!

Events in H's life: sells wife & child when drunk: years later = reformed; gives up alcohol, businessman & mayor: wife & child return - life starts to go wrong, loses business & power; wife dies; Farfrae; turns to drink again; alone & rejected - dies

Don't just look at one bit — you need to write about the whole thing. When you start your plan, make sure you start by giving an answer to the question.

Two things to blame for H's downfall - his own character & Fate
- **own character** - sold his wife, and his mistake haunts him
  treats people badly - selfish - afraid of losing Eliz. so lies to her
  jealous of Farfrae - isolates himself - makes things worse
- **Fate** - gen. change in trading methods ruins Henchard = chance:
  but also, everything that could go wrong does go wrong

You've got to find specific bits of the book to write about, but you've also got to keep the whole thing in mind. Remember — each of your points needs to back up your answer.

A library bus — bringing people to book...

Novel essays can be difficult to plan — you have to find a balance between writing about specific bits to back up your points, and writing about the whole book. The main thing is to answer the question.

Planning Play Essays

How To Plan Essays On Plays

The secret of planning your writing about plays is simple — don't just write down what happens. You've got to answer the question by explaining why it happens.

Remember To Answer The Points From The Question

Use the points from the question to help you make your plan.

> What do you think is the most important theme in *Death of a Salesman*?
> You may wish to consider:
> - the way Willy talks about his life
> - the change in Biff's character between the past and the present
> - the hidden secrets of the family
> - the dreams of the main characters.

First you need to decide what all the main themes are — then you can choose the most important one.

Start By Jotting Down Rough Notes For Each Point

Each note answers one of the points from the question.

Even I jot down rough notes.

Most Important Theme - Death of a Salesman

1) Willy = always hopeful; looking to future: says life = better than it is: deceives self - can't face truth - knows he's failure but pretends not to be - doesn't fit in the modern world
2) Biff = was great hero - quarterback - typical success story BUT found out about affair - dropped-out; stopped trying - can't stand authority - doesn't fit in the system
3) Willy's affair casts shadow over all family - ruined Biff's life, & now Willy desp. to make it up to him - but too proud...

Put Your Main Point First In Your Final Plan

You need to choose your main point from your notes. Start your final plan with it to answer the question.

Most important theme in D.o.a.S is how the modern world destroys people who don't fit in the system
1 - Willy believes in American Dream - believes he can be a success - but he isn't - so he thinks he's a failure & kills himself.
2 - Biff doesn't believe in Dream - thinks it's a lie - he doesn't fit in the system - can't get a job or be content, like his brother Happy...

Remember — main point first.

You've got to use your other notes to back up your your ideas in the rest of the essay plan.

SECTION THREE — PLANNING YOUR ESSAY

Planning Poetry Essays

How To Plan A Poetry Essay

Watch out — you need to give lots of <u>detail</u> when you're writing <u>poetry essays</u>. Poems are <u>shorter</u> than plays or novels, so the examiners <u>expect</u> you to read them <u>more closely</u>.

Planning *Poetry* Essays Means *Reading Closely*

What makes "The Darkling Thrush" by Thomas Hardy such a powerful poem? You should consider:
- Hardy's use of words and images
- the setting and atmosphere
- what the poem is about.

You've got to work out <u>as many</u> things <u>as possible</u> to write about — to do that you need to <u>read</u> the poem over and over, <u>scribbling down</u> any <u>key points</u>. Think about <u>language</u>, <u>mood</u>, <u>images</u>, "<u>plot</u>" and <u>hidden meanings</u>.

- <u>images</u> of frost, cold & death- ghost <u>words</u> - "spectres", "spirits", "haunted" etc.
- <u>bleak setting</u>: landscape = like a corpse - dead body of century - graveyard feel - everything = lifeless
- birdsong suddenly <u>changes</u> things - brave old bird "flings soul into gloom" : <u>contrast</u> between <u>bleak</u> landscape and the <u>happy</u> song - perhaps the bird knows something about Hope that the poet doesn't

TWEET!

You Need To Write About *How* The Poem *Makes You Feel*

You must put down <u>your opinions</u> when you're asked a question about why a poem is <u>powerful</u> or <u>good</u>. Then you need to <u>use</u> the <u>details</u> you've picked up from your <u>close reading</u> to help you <u>plan</u>.

The poem = powerful <u>because</u> it creates <u>bleak atmosphere</u> of winter & death but gives <u>image of hope</u> in song of thrush
— v. vivid descriptions - ghosts and old age - death, shrunken, tired, "haunted", "spectres", "spirits" etc
— land seemed like "Century's corpse" = esp. vivid - feeling that progress has stopped & whole century has died - sense of despair filling the whole world.
— but sudden change - happy song in midst of gloom and despair about the future - something hopeful in song

<u>Back up</u> your opinions with <u>words</u> and <u>images</u> from the poem.

You've <u>also</u> got to try to <u>explain</u> what the images <u>mean</u>.

SQUAWK!

This poem isn't for softies — it was written by Hardy...

Poems always <u>look like</u> an easy option — but they <u>aren't</u>. You have to read them much <u>more closely</u>, especially the images. Remember that the <u>images</u> in a poem may <u>not</u> be completely clear the <u>first time</u> you read it. If that happens, you'll have to <u>read it again</u> until you're sure you <u>understand</u> it.

SECTION THREE — PLANNING YOUR ESSAY

How To Plan Comparisons

This is where you need to concentrate — if you can get comparing straight, you're onto a winner. Just remember this — you've got to write about similarities and differences between things.

Use This Same Method Whatever You're Comparing

1) Start by working out what the question is asking for.

> Compare two poems from the selection which are about people and their environment. You might like to consider:
> - what each poem is about
> - how the poems use words and phrases
> - what the poems say about people and their surroundings
> - reasons why you like/dislike the poems.

My environment's a bit nippy pal.

2) You must use these four suggestions as the main points for your plan.

Go Through Each Poem In Turn And Make Notes

You've got to scribble an answer to each point of the question.

I don't like wind either! Aaah!

Edward Thomas: "The New House"

— poem = about going into a new house - wind howls & makes house feel old - as if you can feel what the future will be like
— language - short and mysterious words - all horrible things 'grief', 'storm': strange rhythm makes you feel scared - one long line then a short line, sounds like the wind blowing
— poem says people can pick up emotion from a place - wind plays tricks on imagination & makes you think -
— don't like it = v. uncomfortable poem - nothing happy in the future... well written but don't like.

Here you can use "I" to give a personal answer — the question asks you to.

Read the poems carefully and scribble your answers in rough. Then do the same thing with the other poem.

Gerard Manley Hopkins: "Spring and Fall"

— poem = about young girl upset by autumn - trees losing leaves in a place called Goldengrove
— language = v difficult : lines rhyme in pairs, lots of words about fresh things growing old, and 'sorrow'
— poem says that girl is crying now, but when she's older she won't cry at these things - she will get used to sorrow - she isn't really crying for the leaves but for herself getting old
— like it - sad poem but very beautiful - poet sees beauty in girl's sadness, and knows what it means.

Each note is an answer to one of the question points.

More On Planning Comparisons

SIMILARITIES & DIFFERENCES

Don't start your essay yet — you haven't finished planning it. When you've looked at both poems, you need to work out how to compare the facts you've found out.

You've Got To Look At Similarities And Differences

Go through each point from the question in turn, and write down your answers side by side.

Poems on people & their environment

"The New House"
ABOUT going to new place - suddenly feeling strange atmosphere - the sad things to come in the future: sad and scary poem

"Spring and Fall"
ABOUT seeing well-known place changing - how young girl is upset but older people aren't, because they're used to changes - they're changing with age too. Sad poem.

It's a great way to compare the two poems — but you're still not finished yet. You need to write a quick list of similarities and differences between the poems.

Similarities
1) Both poems = about how places can bring out different emotions in people
2) Both poems = about growing older
3) Both poems = sad tone

Differences
1) "New H." = sad & scary - "Sp. & Fall" is sad
2) "Sp. & Fall" is to a child, about her feelings; "New H." = writing about his own feelings
3) "New H." is about a new place; 'Sp. & Fall' isn't

You Must Match Up The Similarities In Your Final Plan

Make sure each point in your plan answers one of the points from the question.

a) Both poems about how places bring out emotions in people
b) Explain what New H. = about. Then what Sp. & Fall = about
c) Poems have big difference - NH is the same person, S&F is an older person talking to the girl
d) Both poems about getting older - realising that things change - special places start people thinking...
e) Language used in NH = simple but strange and spooky; in S&F = simple because it's spoken to a child - v. pretty... etc...

You're answering points 1) and 3) here.

This answers point 1).

And you need these ones to answer point 2).

Remember to put in all the similarities and differences, and back them up with examples from the poems.

Similarities — I can't tell the difference, myself...

Don't write about each one separately. Find the similarities and differences and write about both together.

SECTION THREE — PLANNING YOUR ESSAY

| THREE TIPS TO REMEMBER | # Three Big Tips |

These *three tips* are really worth *learning*. You'll definitely *need* to remember them.

Never Start Without Planning Your Writing

1) *Don't rush* into your writing — you're much *more* likely to get *confused* and *make mistakes*.

2) You must *take time* to plan your writing, whether you're doing an *exam* or a piece of *coursework*.

3) Even if the question *looks* easy, it's *still* important to make a plan. You *don't* want to *miss* a key point out of your answer — *especially* if it's an *easy* question where you *could* pick up *high marks*.

4) *Don't worry* about what *other people* do — particularly in exams. Just concentrate on making *your* writing *clear*... by *planning* it first.

I started writing without a plan, and look what happened to me!

Don't Contradict Yourself

Look at this sentence. It *doesn't* make sense — you'd *lose marks* if you wrote it in an essay.

Magwitch is a good man, but he is very cruel and wicked.

The idea of '*good*' and the idea of '*cruel*' and '*wicked*' are complete *opposites*. This a *contradiction*.

CONTRADICTING yourself = saying one thing and then saying exactly the opposite.

1) You've got to *watch out* for contradictions in the *different points* of your plan.

2) You'll *lose* loads of *marks* if you put them in your writing by *mistake*.

3) Make sure your *whole essay* makes *sense*, and *anyone* reading it can *understand* it.

4) *Every point* of your plan has to *follow on* clearly from the *last* one.

Always Tell The Examiners What You're Doing

This is going to sound *weird*, but it's true. The *big reason* for planning is so that *you know* what you're *going to write*, and you can make it *clear*. The only way to do that is to *tell* the examiners *exactly* what you're doing. This comes up in *detail* on pages 44 and 45, but for now *learn* this:

Pretend the examiners are *thick*, and you have to be *really clear* or they *won't understand* your writing.

Don't contradict yourself — it sounds painful...

Time to get these three tips *learned*. They're all about *keeping your head* when you write, instead of rushing in and messing things up. The *bottom line* is if you can *plan* your work *calmly*, you'll *do well*.

SECTION THREE — PLANNING YOUR ESSAY

Revision Summary

Phew — a whopper of a section. Planning essays won't set your socks on fire with excitement, but it can make a SERIOUS difference to the quality of your work. It's all about organising ideas, so that you get them in order and don't repeat yourself. That's bound to help you get the marks. The only way to make sure that you've got it all sorted in your head, is to do every last one of these questions. Go over the section again and again (and again) until you know it all.

1) Why is it a good idea to plan?
2) How can you use the question to help you plan your argument?
3) When should you write notes of the important bits to include?
   a) before you write the plan b) twice daily after meals
4) What do you need from the text to back up the points of your argument?
5) What are the steps you follow to make your final plan?
6) You should always double check that your plan matches
    a) the curtains b) the question c) your handbag.
7) How do you go about planning an English (not English literature) essay?
8) When the question tells you a load of points to write about, in what order should you write about them?
9) How can you use your own experiences in story writing?
10) What things do you need to think about when you're deciding what a story's going to be about?
11) In what way is starting a story in the middle of the action a good idea?
12) Why do you have to keep stories short?
13) With planning essays about novels, do you have to think about the whole book or just one bit?
14) When you plan a play essay, you shouldn't just write down what happens. What else should you do?
15) What does planning poetry essays involve?
16) In a poetry essay plan, is putting how you feel about the poem
    a) a good idea b) a rubbish idea?
17) When you're comparing two things, should you just write about the similarities? If not, what else should you write about?
18) Put these in the right order:
    a) Go through each point from the question in turn, and write down your answers side by side.
    b) Write a quick list of similarities and differences between the poems.
    c) Go through each poem/article you're comparing and write notes
19) When is it a good idea to write without planning first? a) always b) never c) about 9.13 pm
20) You shouldn't contradict yourself. What does that mean?
21) Would you tell a mate not to bother being clear in the exams, because the examiners will figure it out somehow? If you did, would they thank you?

Imelda loved to plane her writing.

SECTION THREE — PLANNING YOUR ESSAY

SECTION FOUR — STARTING YOUR WRITING

How To Write An Opening Line

Starting An Essay

Starting essays is horrible. It's one of the hardest things about them.
You need to remember one important piece of advice — get to the point right away.

You Need To Do Three Things In Your Opening Line

1) You must get to the point straightaway.
2) You must make sure your answer fits the question.
3) You must grab the attention of anyone reading it.

I bet I grabbed your attention.

Get To The Point — Don't Waste Time

1) First, you need to work out what the question is asking you to do.

> Which of the boys in *Lord of the Flies* do you think would have been the best leader?

2) That's easy. It's asking you to think about which boy you think would have been the best leader. Plan your essay by thinking about why some of the different boys would have been good leaders.

3) When you've planned your essay, you've could start it by giving a clear answer to the question. Just give your opinion immediately — but keep it impersonal (don't use "I"). The rest of the essay will be about backing it up with examples.

> *Ralph would have been the best leader, because he is the one who realises that the boys are losing their self-control.*

They should follow me, I'm so brainy!
Brain-o-matic
No you ain't!

4) Be careful — you can't always give a direct answer at the beginning. The question may be too tricky, or perhaps you can't make up your mind yet.

> *Several of the boys have features that would have made them a good leader; Piggy's intelligence, Jack's strength, Ralph's common sense and Simon's courage.*

5) This doesn't give an immediate answer, but it shows you're trying to answer the question. The rest of the essay would be about the good and bad features of each boy as a leader.

Begin a beheading early — get a head start...

Beginning your work is always going to be tricky. Never start an essay with a long introduction. If you want good marks, you have to show the examiners you're getting to the point right away.

Your Opening Paragraph

How To Write An Opening Paragraph

Your first sentence is important, but so is the rest of your opening paragraph.
It needs to kick start your essay, showing that you're really going to answer the question.

It Must Follow On From The Opening Sentence

> What is the effect of the first person narrative in *Great Expectations*?

This question's asking you about the fact that Pip tells you the story himself. You've got to give a clear answer in the opening sentence.

Then you need to explain what you mean.

> Pip's first person narrative makes you feel as though you're inside his head. You see things the way he saw them when he was a child. When he goes to steal food for the convict in Chapter Two, he describes his childish fear vividly: "I got up and went down stairs; every board upon the way, and every crack in every board, calling after me, 'Stop thief!' and 'Get up Mrs Joe!'"

You have to back up your point by giving some kind of example, like this.

The examiner will see straightaway that you're trying to answer the question.

Use The Exact Question Words In The First Paragraph

'Ant Spectacles'?

> Do you think that *An Inspector Calls* is just an interesting detective story that keeps you guessing?

If you use the exact question words in your first paragraph, it shows you're answering the question.

> *An Inspector Calls* is more than just an interesting detective story. It keeps you guessing, but not only about Eva's death and who is responsible. It soon becomes clear that everyone is responsible in different ways. The Inspector's questions make the characters look at their actions and realise that they have ruined the life of another person.

The paragraph gives a clear answer, which will lead on to the rest of your essay.

Essays are like heavy doors — open them carefully...

Opening paragraphs are a pain in the neck. They aren't just something you can scribble down in a hurry. The examiners start judging your work as soon as they read it. You've got to show you understand the question and that you're giving a clear answer. Try to use the exact question words.

Section Four — Starting Your Writing

STARTING FORMAL & INFORMAL LETTERS

Starting Other Kinds of Answer

The thing is, essays aren't the only kind of answer you'll have to write. Sometimes you need to write letters, reports and articles as well.

You Must Start Letters Properly

① A friend has written you a letter saying she/he is planning to run away and asking for your advice. Write a reply trying to **persuade** her/him not to run away.

This question is asking you to write to a friend. You need to start the letter in the same way you'd write to a real friend.

Give the date. → Monday 23rd May

Dear Paul,

   I got your letter yesterday, and I couldn't believe it. What are you doing mate? Running away isn't going to solve your problems with Louise.

Use casual language because Paul's your friend.

But don't forget — you still need to get to the point in your first paragraph.

② Your school has decided to stop providing meals at lunchtime. Write a letter to the headteacher in favour of keeping school meals.

Here you've got to write a formal letter, using clear formal language.

It is equally acceptable to put your name and address at the top left of your letter rather than the top right.

Give your name, address and the date. →

Jane Smith
Student Council
Thursday 14 June

Mrs Oates
Headteacher's Office

Give the name and address of whoever you're writing to.

Dear Mrs Oates,

Begin by explaining why you're writing.

   I am writing to express my concerns about the decision to end school meals. For many students here, it is the only healthy meal they eat all day.

Make sure you get to the point in the first paragraph.

Letters can be expensive — they start off 'dear'...

It's all pretty boring stuff this, but you really need to get it clear in your mind. Letters aren't that difficult to write, as long as you remember two things: who you're writing to, and whether you've got to be formal or not. Make sure you learn and practise how to start both kinds of letter properly.

Starting Articles And Reports

How To Begin Articles/Reports

A lot of English questions ask you to write articles for different kinds of magazine or newsletter, or reports for a particular group of people.

The Style Of An Article Should Fit The Situation

This is where it gets tricky. You're being marked on two things here — how well you answer the question, and how well you write in the style of a real article.

> Your school has raised money to help refugees from a war-torn country. Write an **article** for your school newspaper about why you think this charity is important.

You need to write in a punchy style, like a newspaper. You could even start with a headline.

> Why Refugees Matter.
>
> Imagine if you were treated so badly at home that you had to run away. Imagine living in the middle of a war, afraid you might be killed at any second. That's what many refugees have to go through, and that's why our school has been raising money to help refugee charities.

You've got to grab people's attention like a real newspaper article.

You also have to get to the point quickly.

Getting the style right is hard. Think about who you're writing for — people at school or parents etc.

Reports Are About Giving Facts And Opinions

> The local council want to make the road outside your school safer. There are three plans: a ban on all cars along the road during school hours, reducing the speed limit or putting in speed bumps.
>
> Write a **report** for the council in which you explain the advantages and disadvantages of each of the three plans.

Your answer needs to sound like a formal report, so you need to put exactly what it's about in the first paragraph — that means mentioning both the advantages and the disadvantages.

> Each of the three plans proposed would help to make the school road safer. Unfortunately, they would also have a major effect on traffic all around the town. The first suggestion is...

Make sure you give all the important information you can think of about what the plans are.

Section Four — Starting Your Writing

How To Start Descriptions

Starting Descriptions

Descriptions are a lot harder to start. They don't always give you a clear question to answer. The trick is to grab the examiners' attention and show that you know what you're doing.

You Can Be Asked To Describe Things From Extracts

1) This is all about reading the extracts properly first — see Section Seven.

When you said you had a frog in your throat...

> Write about the doctor and the medicine man.
> You should include:
> - what they do
> - how they are different
> - how the writers use words to describe them

2) These are the things you have to put in your answer.
   Put them in at the start, and you'll show you're going to answer the question.

3) You can start off by giving a quick description of what they do.

> Both the doctor and the medicine man are shown as healers. The doctor is a scientist, who uses technology and logic to try to heal people. The medicine man is different because...

4) Then you should go on to say how they are different.

Sometimes You Need To Describe What You Think

Here you have to describe what you think about someone or something.

> Describe the character of someone you look up to, and explain why you look up to them.

You need to start by saying who you're going to write about and why.

> Martin Luther King was an amazing man. He stood up for black people's rights even though he knew the risks.
> People look up to him because he never showed his fear in the most dangerous moments, like the marches in Alabama.

Then you've got to start describing his character in detail, and explaining why you look up to him.

Police stole my homework — they took my description...

Articles, reports and descriptions are a hassle. They don't follow a nice easy pattern like the beginnings of essays. You've really got to work out who you're writing for — the start of an article for a teenage magazine will be very different from a school newspaper article, or an official report.

Starting Stories

How To Start A Story

One last thing in this section — make sure you learn it carefully.
Some English questions may ask you to write a story. This is much more difficult than it sounds.

Stories Don't Have Rules To Follow

The big problem with writing stories is that you don't have a set of rules to follow.
All you can do is try to keep the reader interested, and make the story come to life.

100000 Volts brought me to life...

Start Your Story In The Middle Of The Action

Write a story about a time when you wish you had acted differently.

Yawn!

NO!

Don't start off being boring, or you'll lose marks straightaway.

Once, many years ago, when I was a lot younger, we were on holiday in Spain. There were all sorts of exciting things there, and we were having a really good time.

This is seriously dull. It doesn't jump out at you or grab your attention.

Here's a better example. It starts right in the middle of the action.

Oi!

I couldn't believe it. He was gone. "He must be here somewhere," I thought to myself, as I went through the shed, desperately picking up boxes and throwing them aside. It was no use. Peter had run away again, and it was all my fault.

1) Straight from the first sentence, you want to know what's going on.
2) The person telling the story sounds really worried, which makes the story exciting.
3) You only find out what has happened at the end of the first paragraph.
4) The last sentence makes it clear that the story is about "a time when you wish you had acted differently". It shows that the story is definitely answering the question.

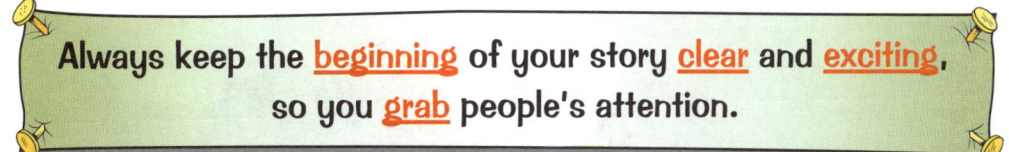

> Always keep the beginning of your story clear and exciting, so you grab people's attention.

My house is made of books — it's ten stories high...

Get this straight now. Stories aren't an easy option. They aren't like essays where you win marks for trying to answer the question. You're being marked on how well you write — especially at the start.

SECTION FOUR — STARTING YOUR WRITING

Revision Summary

The examiners will already be making up their minds about your mark when they've read your first paragraph. You've got to show them you're answering the question, or they'll think you don't understand it. The secret is to keep your opening paragraph as clear as possible. Have a go at these revision questions, and keep doing it till you get things straight.

1) What are the features of a good opening line to an essay?
2) My mate Henryka reckons that "not giving your opinion straight away and waiting till the end instead" is the best way to give a direct answer. Is she right?
3) If you started with an opinion, what would you do for the rest of the essay?
4) What do you have to do if you can't give an opinion straight away?
5) What would the rest of that essay (in Q4) be about?
6) How can you show the examiners that you're answering the question in your first paragraph?
7) Why should you use the exact question words in your answer?
8) The reason you should always check who you're writing to, is to see if the letter should be *a)* written on paper or balloons *b)* formal or informal *c)* mashed with a fork. a), b) or c)?
9) How do you start a letter to a friend properly?
10) Write the beginning, and the first paragraph of a letter to your best friend, telling him or her about a strange day. Make sure you start it properly.
11) How do you start a formal letter properly?
12) Write the beginning, and the first paragraph of a letter to the editor of the free local newspaper, complaining about the amount of paper that free newspapers waste.
13) When they mark articles, examiners are particularly looking for how well you answer the question, and one other thing. What is the other thing?
14) Write the opening paragraph of an article about exam stress for a teenage magazine. Write about the pressures of exams and the importance of results. Make sure you think about the style you should be writing in.
15) When you have to write a report, should it be formal, informal, or all in Greek?
16) Write the opening paragraph of a report for your school governors on why your school needs more sport. Write about the things students learn from sport, like teamwork, as well as problems like fitting it into a busy school day. Think about who you're writing for.
17) Write the opening paragraph of a description of your favourite place. Make sure it's clear.
18) Write the opening paragraph of a description of your best friend. Make sure it's clear.
19) Should you: *a)* start your story in the middle of the action,
    or   *b)* take ages and ages waffling on before anything interesting at all happens?

Start an essay? They couldn't even start their cars.

Section Four — Starting Your Writing

SECTION FIVE — ARGUING YOUR CASE

How To Argue
How To Create An Argument

Talk about strange — most of the writing you've got to do for English or English Literature is a form of arguing. You need to make a series of clear points that form an answer to the question.

You've Got To Carry On From The Opening Paragraph

1) Remember — you need to say what you're writing about in your opening paragraph.

> What qualities make *The Mayor of Casterbridge* a good novel?

2) Get to the point straightaway. You must explain exactly what you mean.

> *The Mayor of Casterbridge* is a good novel because Henchard's character is so vivid. Even though Henchard behaves cruelly for most of the book, Hardy still makes us feel sorry for him. All the way through the book we feel as though we know exactly what Henchard is going through.

3) Now comes the hard part — you've got to carry on with your answer. The only way is to keep explaining your answer, giving reasons to back it up.

> This is because Hardy shows us in clear detail how Henchard's life falls apart. All his emotions are brought to life, so that we feel that he is a real person. In Chapter XVI, Henchard sacks his manager because he is jealous of him. Later Hardy tells us, "his heart sank within him at what he had said and done."

4) As well as giving reasons, you need examples to back up your points.

You Must Use Your Plan When You Write Your Essay

If you want to get good marks, you must follow your plan.
All you need to do is follow the points of your plan, and make sure you explain each one properly.

> Henchard's fear of being left alone - buys a wedding present for Elizabeth-Jane - leaves rather than ruin wedding: why?

You need to turn your notes into something the Examiners can read and understand.

Carry On Arguing — I don't think I saw that one...

English is all about arguing — it's weird but it's true. You've got to persuade the examiners that they should give you lots of lovely marks. That means using your plan to write a clear argument.

ARGUING TO SUPPORT YOUR ANSWER

Answering The Question

I know this is boring, but it's extremely important — your essay must fit the question. Unfortunately, that's not as easy as it sounds.

There Are No Right Answers In English Or English Lit.

You need to keep this in mind when you're writing an essay.
None of the questions you're asked will have one right answer. Instead there are possible answers.

But Remember These Two Things

1) That doesn't mean you can write down any old rubbish. Even though the questions don't have right answers, you can still give wrong answers.

2) The only way to make sure you don't give a wrong answer is to back up your points with evidence and examples.

Look for the evidence.

You Must Concentrate On Backing Up Your Answer

Prove it!

There isn't a right answer to a question like this one.

> What part does conflict play in *Romeo and Juliet*?

The examiners can't just decide if your answer is right or wrong straightaway. They'll give you marks for how well you back up your case.

> In *Romeo and Juliet*, the conflict between the Montagues and the Capulets is what causes the tragedy. Romeo and Juliet are never free to love each other without the feud between their families getting in the way.

That's why you've got to argue in support of your answer — you need to give evidence to back up your points.

> The clearest example of this is when Tybalt challenges Romeo to fight him in Act III, scene i. Romeo loves Juliet, and refuses to fight her cousin. Tybalt does not accept this, and fights and kills Mercutio. When his friend is killed, there is nothing Romeo can do except fight Tybalt. Even when Romeo doesn't want to fight, he ends up being dragged into the conflict.

As long as you can back up your answer properly, it won't be wrong.

The better you back up your answer, the better your marks will be.

Questions from the left — no right answers...

There are no exact right answers in English — it's all about how you back up your case.

SECTION FIVE — ARGUING YOUR CASE

Following Your Plan

MAKING SURE YOU FOLLOW YOUR PLAN

If you're going to explain your points clearly, you've got to use your plan.
It'll help you make sure you don't leave any important ideas out.

Follow Your Plan And Link Your Points Together

Your plan should give you all the key information you need for your answer.
The hard part is turning your notes into a clear argument that the examiner can follow.

1) You should start by making sure that you follow your plan.
   Try to keep your points in the same order.

   > What qualities interest you in Wordsworth's poetry?

   > PLAN
   > 1) nature images for grief - Lucy as a flower - ii) violet by mossy stone: iv) "lovelier flower" never sown on earth
   > 2) descriptions of places - real places they went to i); places she will go after death iv) - nature descriptions - Lucy always connected to nature - part of it - esp. v) she has become part of natural cycle.
   > 3) interesting language.

2) Don't forget — your points have to answer the question.

3) Every time you start a new point, start a new paragraph — it makes your argument clearer.

   > Wordsworth's poems about Lucy are interesting because of the way he uses images of nature to express his grief at her death. His love for her is expressed in an image of her as a flower in poems ii) and iv), that makes her death seem all the more real.
   >
   > Wordsworth *also* uses descriptions of places, such as forests, fields and orchards to show Lucy's relationship with nature. <u>Both of these techniques make the language of the poem more intense and more emotional</u>.

   New point, new paragraph.

4) Your plan is just a shopping list. You'll always get more marks if you can follow a set of points with a further comment 'linking' them in some way. You only need one good cross-link, preferably relevant to the main theme (in this case "interesting language" perhaps).

Arguing with a wasp — better follow Plan Bee...

Following your plan is a good way to keep your essay clear — as long as you made a proper plan in the first place (see Section Three). Remember — every time you start a new point, you should start a new paragraph. And make sure you link your points together carefully too.

SECTION FIVE — ARGUING YOUR CASE

Making It Clear

KEEPING YOUR ARGUMENT CLEAR

Writing an essay is all about making things perfectly clear for anyone reading. You need to learn these tricks carefully and make sure you use them in your work.

You Must Use The Key Words From The Question

1) Here are the key words in the question.

> Choose two of Blake's poems that have something important to say. Explain what the important ideas are in each poem, and how Blake brings these ideas out.

2) The best way to make it clear to the examiners that you've definitely answered the question is to keep using these key words all the way through your argument.

> The important idea in "London" is how people find themselves trapped by their lives and by their imaginations. Blake brings this out by talking about the "mind-forged manacles". The words "mind-forged" mean something created in the mind, and "manacles" are chains, so the image means "the chains in people's imaginations". This is a very vivid image.
>
> Another important idea in the poem is how...

Key words!

3) Remember — using the key words shows the examiners that your points are relevant to the question.

Explain What You're Doing Clearly

This is where you really need to think. Whenever you write an essay, you need to give examples and you need to explain what you're doing.

Explain what you're doing.
I just felt like a spin...

Examples are bits of evidence that back up your points — see Section Six.

> In the third stanza, Blake writes that the soldier's sigh, "Runs in blood down palace walls".

Explaining means making sure the examiners understand what your points and examples mean.

> He uses this image to show his opinion that the people in the palace (the King and his ministers) are really the ones responsible for the deaths of soldiers in wars, because they make the decisions. This is an important idea to Blake — the way that ordinary people's lives are destroyed by the people who are in power.

Don't just write down what happens — you must explain why your example is relevant to the question.

SECTION FIVE — ARGUING YOUR CASE

Using Clear Language

USING FORMAL LANGUAGE

This is a surefire trick to make your argument easy to understand — keep the language simple. Pretend that the examiners are really stupid. The only way they'll understand is if you explain exactly what you're doing in plain, formal language. Of course, they aren't really...

You Must Write In Formal Language

Any essay you write needs to be in formal language. That doesn't mean it's got to be full of posh long words — you just need to think about who you're writing for.

Keep your writing simple and formal, as if you're talking to a teacher.

Use phrases like "at the same time" to make your writing more interesting.

> The poem is full of images of suffering. Blake seems to see suffering as the main feature of human life. At the same time, he makes it clear that he believes that London itself is the cause of a lot of this suffering.

Write about the author and the poem in the present, unless it's about an actual historical event.

'Formal luggage!'
The key point is that... ...the author's works are... ...full of strong images.

> Don't use abbreviations like "it's" or "you're", and don't use slang words — you'll lose marks if you do.

You Should Also Use Clear Explaining Words And Phrases

You've got to use explaining words and phrases to make your essay easy to follow.

- This means that...
- This is because...
- The problem with this is....
- Another key point is...
- The important thing is...

Make it clear...

You must use these phrases to help you explain what your points mean. And remember — there are plenty more phrases like these you can use as well.

You Can Also Use Negative Phrases

- This doesn't mean that...
- This isn't the same as...

Explaining words — a phrase I'm going through...

Explaining your points will win you good marks — it shows the examiners that you understand the question and that you're answering it properly. The key to explaining your points is using the right kind of language in your writing. Make sure you keep your argument formal — don't use slang words and definitely don't swear. Practise using explaining phrases — start by learning the ones here.

SECTION FIVE — ARGUING YOUR CASE

| How To Link Points Together | # Linking Words |

We're not quite finished with words yet. The other trick you need to practise is using linking words. These are the lovely helpful words that link different points of your essay together.

You Need To Link Different Points Together

Don't just jump from one point to the next — you need to show the examiners that your essay is organised.
For example, you can divide your work up into numbered points.

> There are three main points... Firstly... Secondly... Finally....

Make sure you start a new paragraph for each numbered point.

Start Every Paragraph With A Different Linking Word

Furthermore...   Nevertheless...

Although...   Instead...

Don't forget these useful phrases too.

Another view is....   Even though...

Despite this...   At the same time...

Linking? I thought you said Lincoln...

You Can Also Use Opposite Phrases

Sometimes when you're arguing, you need to give two sides. That's when you should use phrases like these.

On the one hand...   On the other hand....   One way...   Another way...

This could mean...   Alternatively, it might mean...

Use However And Therefore In The Middle Of Sentences

This means, therefore, that...   Another view, however, is that...

Linking — isn't that in Lincolnshire...

Linking words are pretty boring — but there's no way around them. They're the perfect way to stick your essay together. That's bound to impress the examiners and win you some valuable marks.

SECTION FIVE — ARGUING YOUR CASE

Two-Sided Arguments

A BALANCED ARGUMENT

Writing an essay <u>isn't</u> just about saying <u>what you think</u> and nothing else.
You've <u>also</u> got to be able to give <u>different sides</u> of the argument.

You Have To Give Different Sides For Some Answers

1) Watch out — this question <u>doesn't</u> have a <u>simple right answer</u>.
<u>Instead</u> you need to give as many <u>different ideas</u> as you can.

> As a senior student, write an advice sheet for pupils joining your school. Give them helpful advice on how to survive.

2) The <u>easiest</u> way to <u>answer</u> this question is to write a <u>two-sided</u> argument. <u>Start</u> your answer by explaining <u>both sides</u> of your argument.

3) Next make a <u>clear point</u> for <u>one side</u> of the argument.

4) Then make a point for the <u>other side</u>.

> You need to know two important things when you join this school — <u>what to do</u>, and <u>what not to do</u>. If you can learn them at the start, you will have a great time here.
>
> The first thing to say is <u>don't</u> be scared. Things will be different and they'll take some getting used to.
>
> <u>Do</u> feel free to ask questions, though. Everybody may look scary, but they aren't really...

I'm not scary...

5) This way your argument will move between <u>positive</u> things and <u>negative</u> things. It'll also be very <u>easy</u> for the examiners to <u>follow</u>, which will help you pick up some <u>big marks</u>.

> <u>Don't</u> write all about <u>one side</u> of the argument <u>before</u> the other.
> Write about <u>both</u> of them <u>together</u>.

Give Both Sides When You Can't Make Up Your Mind

You've got <u>two options</u> here. <u>Either</u> you can make up your mind, or you can argue <u>both sides</u> of the question.

> Is Macbeth a wholly evil character? Give reasons for your answer.

If you're arguing <u>both sides</u>, you need to give your reasons <u>for</u> and <u>against</u> the statement.

I can see both sides...

> Macbeth can be seen as a <u>wholly evil person</u>, so greedy for power that he is willing to murder anyone who gets in his way. <u>On the other hand</u>, he can also be seen as a <u>good man</u> who makes one mistake, and finds himself sucked into committing worse and worse crimes.

> <u>Remember</u> — there <u>isn't</u> a right answer.
> It's all about <u>backing up</u> what you say.

SECTION FIVE — ARGUING YOUR CASE

How To Change Your Argument | Changing Your Line Of Argument

The biggest nightmare with essays is when you realise that your line of argument is wrong — and you're halfway through writing your answer. That's why you need to read this page.

Don't Cross Out What You've Already Written

1) Don't panic — it's a complete waste of time crossing out what you've written.

2) Stop and think about why your line of argument is wrong.

3) Then carry on from where you left off, explaining to the examiners why what you've said so far is wrong, and what you think your answer should be.

4) You won't lose marks for realising your mistake, and you'll even pick up extra marks for giving a clear explanation.

I can see where I went wrong...

Tell The Examiners You're Changing Your Argument

You must tell the examiners when you decide to change your argument, otherwise it won't make sense to them.

> When he orders the murder of Macduff's wife and children, Macbeth shows clearly that he is wholly evil.
> This isn't entirely true, though. In fact, the argument up to now has missed out some important pieces of evidence.
> When Macbeth orders the murder of Macduff and his family, he does it out of fear. He is afraid — which is a very normal reaction. Also, he orders someone else to do the killing, as if he couldn't do it himself. That is not what a wholly evil person would do.

I'm going to change my mind.

Then you've got to carry on. Start by writing about the things you missed out before.

In Some Opinion Questions, You Can't Change Your Mind

If you're answering a question that asks you for one side or the other, you can't change your argument.

> Write an article for your school newspaper in which you argue either for or against the following statement.

Even if you change your mind halfway through, just carry on arguing for the same side.

Swapping blond ex-boyfriends — a fair ex-change...

Changing your argument is a major hassle. Don't do it unless you really have to. You need to make two things clear — that you were wrong before, but you won't be wrong for the rest of the essay.

SECTION FIVE — ARGUING YOUR CASE

Four Big Tips

FOUR TIPS FOR ARGUING

One last page to go — and it's a yawner. This is pretty dull stuff, but think about it this way — either you learn it and get great marks for your writing, or you don't bother. It's that simple.

Don't Contradict Yourself

You can't put these two opinions in the same essay — they don't make any sense together.

> Macbeth only kills Duncan out of greed for power...
> Macbeth only murders Duncan because his wife forces him...

You're saying that both opinions are the only one — which can't be true. These are opposite opinions. If you want to put both in, don't say they're the only ones.

> One reason Macbeth kills Duncan is because of his greed for power...
> Another reason he murders Duncan is because his wife forces him...

Don't contradict yourself — you'll lose important marks. Always make it clear if you're giving two opposite opinions.

Stick To The Point

Don't get sidetracked — you're only being marked on how well you answer the question. Make sure your essay is clear and sticks to the point.

Keep Your Writing Balanced And Clear

Don't make outrageous statements that you can't back up, and don't be arrogant or rude.

NO!
> There is no way that Macbeth is wholly evil. Anyone who believes that must be stupid.

Now that's well balanced...

You must write a balanced argument, using clear points and plenty of evidence.

Don't Generalise

Whatever you do, don't make sweeping statements like this one.

> All of Shakespeare's plays get boring in Act IV.

It's far too general, and you won't be able to back it up properly. Stick to points you can definitely back up.

Place your bets — four cracking tips here...

Go over this page carefully, and learn these tips. Keep them in mind whenever you're writing essays.

SECTION FIVE — ARGUING YOUR CASE

Revision Summary

The better your arguing skills, the better you'll do in exams and coursework. It's all about making the examiners believe your answer by trying to prove it to them. You've got to be able to write a good argument — so learn the stuff in this section. The best way to test you really know it is to go through all these questions. Make sure you know this section so well you can answer them all without even cheating.

1) Do English and English Literature questions have just one right answer?
2) Can you give *wrong* answers though?
3) If there isn't a right answer to a question, what do you get marks for?
4) How do you back up your answer?
5) Every time you start writing about a new point in your argument, you should also start *a)* a new sentence *b)* a new paragraph *c)* a page.
6) Is it important to make your argument clear to the examiners, or should you let them figure it out for themselves?
7) Why should you use the key words from the question in your argument?
8) My dog Rova doesn't bark. Instead she says "Every time you give an example, you have to explain it." Is she right? If so, in what kind of ways would you explain an example?
9) What kind of language does your argument need to be in?
    a) informal slang *b)* 'proper' formal *c)* Swedish?
10) Is it a OK to use abbreviations like "it's" and "you're"?
11) Which of these things will you lose marks for? *a)* picking your nose *b)* writing in slang *c)* using formal language *d)* using paragraphs *e)* using swear words.
12) You should use explaining words and phrases. How many can you think of?
13) Give six different words or phrases you can use to start a new paragraph.
14) You need 'opposite phrases' when you're giving two sides of an argument. Give three examples of opposite phrases.
15) Is it best to use "however" or "therefore" at the beginning, middle, or end of a sentence?
16) How should you write a two-sided argument?
17) When do you need to write two-sided arguments?
18) If you suddenly realise that your argument is wrong, should you cross it all out?
19) What should you do if you decide your argument is wrong?
20) Why can't you change your argument for some opinion questions? What do you do instead?
21) How do you avoid contradicting yourself?
22) What's the problem with generalising?

Gill thought she'd improve her marks by arguing <u>with</u> her <u>case</u>.

SECTION FIVE — ARGUING YOUR CASE

SECTION SIX — QUOTING & EXAMPLES

Why You Need Examples

BACKING UP YOUR ARGUMENT

Don't just jot down any old stuff — you've got to back it up to get the marks.

You Need To Back Up Your Argument

Writing a good essay is about backing up your points with proper evidence. Otherwise you end up writing amazingly boring, general points.

> In Lord of the Flies, Piggy wouldn't have been a good leader because he is really annoying. Even Ralph finds him annoying sometimes, but not as much as Jack does.

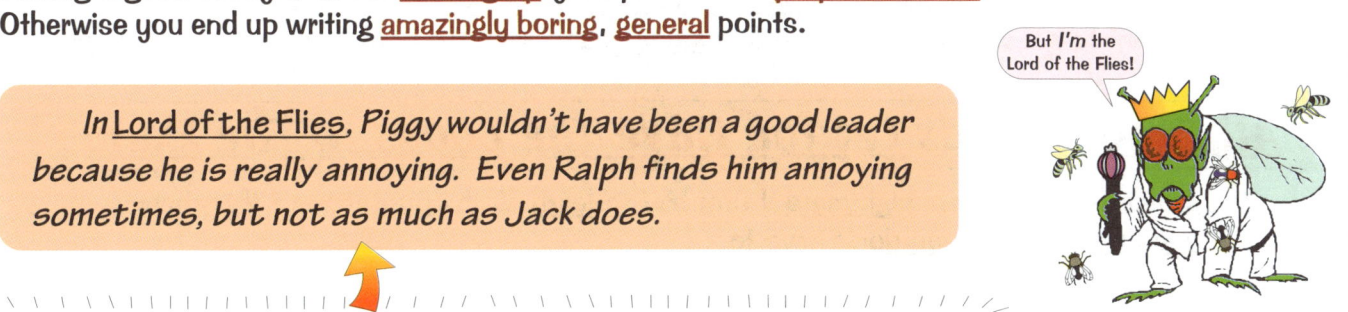

But I'm the Lord of the Flies!

This isn't clear enough. You need evidence of why Piggy's annoying to back up your point.

There Are Two Ways To Back Up Your Points

1) Quoting

Quoting means giving examples from a book, play or poem in the exact same words as the original.

> Frankenstein's monster blames his violent actions on his creator. "I was benevolent and good; misery made me a fiend." (Chapter 10) The monster says that he was good when he was created. When his creator, Frankenstein, rejected him, his loneliness and sadness made him evil.

After you quote something, you have to explain how it backs up your argument.

2) Other Examples

> People buy lottery tickets because they believe they can win. In fact, they're wasting their money. *According to the odds given by the bookmakers, you have more chance of being struck by lightning than winning the jackpot.*

Stick in any other bits of information that are relevant to your essay. You can put these in your own words.

Backing up your points — like reversing a train...

This is a seriously important section. If you don't give examples, you'll never get anywhere with your essays. They're the best way to show the examiners you really know what you're on about.

| QUOTING IN THE EXAMS | # Quoting in Literature Essays |

Here's where this quoting examples business really comes in handy.
It's the only way to get great marks for your literature essays.

Quoting Shows You Know The Book Well

Literature essays are all about answering questions on books you've read.
If you want to get the marks, you need to show you've read the book and know what happens.

All Exam Boards Let You Have The Books In The Exam

This would be a complete nightmare if you had to learn all the quotations off by heart.
The good news is that you don't have to.

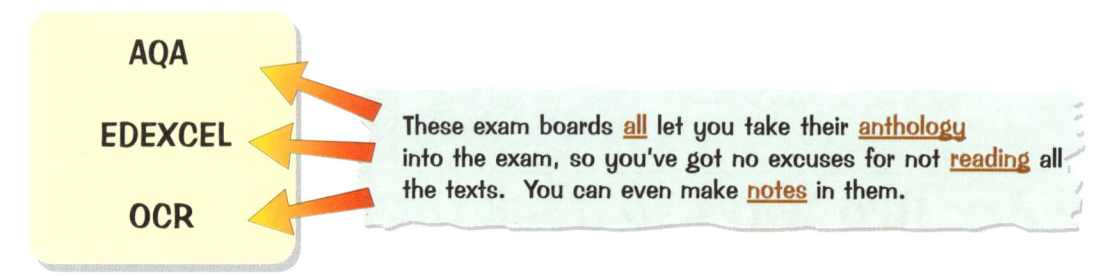

AQA
EDEXCEL
OCR

These exam boards all let you take their anthology into the exam, so you've got no excuses for not reading all the texts. You can even make notes in them.

But — soon you're not going to be allowed to make notes in your books anymore.

You can only use books with notes in them for exams up to and including 2004.

From 2005, books with notes are NOT allowed.

Watch Out Though:

1) Don't make too many notes (if you still can, anyway).

2) You're meant to be relying on your own knowledge of the texts.

3) The whole reason you're allowed to take the anthology in with you, is so that you already know what's coming up.

4) So, for crying out loud, make sure you've read all the texts.

5) You'll look like a right idiot if you don't bother, as everyone else will already know what they're talking about.

6) There — rant over. Just READ all the texts.

Quoting in exams — doing it by the book...

Do I REALLY need to say this again? Of course not. Ruddy well will though. READ THE TEXTS.

Section Six — Quoting & Examples

How to Quote Properly

ENSURING ACCURATE QUOTATION

This quoting stuff is all about being accurate — make sure you learn these tips perfectly.

When You Quote Give The Exact Words Only

1) This is completely wrong. She never actually says it in the book.

   NO! When Boldwood asks Bathsheba to marry him, she says, "Yes."

2) Watch out. She does say this in the book, but it's still wrong...

   When Boldwood asks Bathsheba to marry him, she agrees: "It must be."
   (Far From the Madding Crowd, Chapter 53)

3) ...you've missed out an important bit, which completely changes what the quotation means.

   When Boldwood asks Bathsheba to marry him, she agrees:
   "It must be, I suppose, since you will have it so!"
   (Far From the Madding Crowd, Chapter 53)

4) This is what she actually says. She doesn't say "Yes" — she only agrees because he forces her. Her exact words are very reluctant. You have to quote them properly to make that clear.

> Never add or take away any words from a quotation.
> Give the exact words without changing the meaning.

I'll marry you!

Don't Change The Original Spelling

This spelling looks pretty weird, but you must keep it exactly the same.

You need to do this with old authors, especially Chaucer.

> Ther was also a Nonne, a Prioresse,
> That of hire smylyng was ful symple and coy:
> Hire gretteste ooth was but by Seinte Loy:
>
> The Canterbury Tales: General Prologue, lines 118-120: Geoffrey Chaucer.

Miming omelettes — those eggs-act words...

Quoting can get quite tricky if you don't know the book well. You must make sure you know exactly what the quotation means, and read the bits round about to check. And be really careful not to change the meaning of a quotation. You need the exact words and meaning of the original.

REFERENCING & RELEVANCE

Two Key Rules for Quoting

Getting the right words isn't the end of the story — your quotation has got to be relevant, and you need to say where it came from. That's where you need to stay sharp.

You Must Put Where The Quotation Comes From

"Henchard had chosen this spot as being the safest from observation which he could think of for meeting his long-lost wife."
(The Mayor of Casterbridge: Chapter 11; by Thomas Hardy)

1) The first time you quote from a book, you've got to give the title, the chapter number and the author's name.

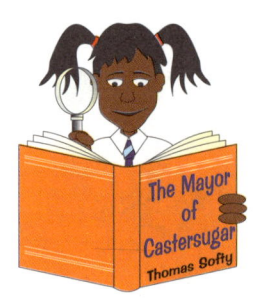

"There, approaching her mother's grave, she saw a solitary dark figure in the middle of the gravel walk." (Chapter 20)

2) Every time you quote from that same book in your essay, just give the chapter number.

"It may have been observed that there is no regular path for getting out of love as there is for getting in."
(Far From the Madding Crowd; Chapter 5)

3) If you quote from another book by the same author, you need the title and the chapter number. If you quote from a book by a different author, then give all the names and titles.

"Heathcliff had knelt on one knee to embrace her; he attempted to rise, but she seized his hair, and kept him down."
(Wuthering Heights; Chapter 15; by Emily Brontë)

Ooch!

Make Sure It's Relevant To Your Point

Here's the point you're making.

Dorian makes excuses for the rumours about his private life by blaming gossip: "In this country it is enough for a man to have distinction and brains for every common tongue to wag against him." (The Picture of Dorian Gray, Chapter 11; Oscar Wilde)

This bit you're quoting is relevant to the point.

Don't quote something just because you know it. It must back up your point.

Quotations and tomatoes — both have sources...

This is dead important. If you want to quote something, you've got to say where it came from.

SECTION SIX — QUOTING & EXAMPLES

When To Use Speech Marks

SPEECH MARKS WITH QUOTATIONS

The trickiest part about quoting is remembering when you need to use speech marks.

You Must Use Speech Marks With Short Quotations

Frankenstein continually talks about his creation as a "monster" or a "devil".

These one word quotations must have speech marks.

You need speech marks with all short quotations — from novels, articles, plays or poems.

Use Speech Marks When You Quote From Novels

Here's a paragraph from an essay about <u>The Mayor of Casterbridge</u>, by Hardy.

This is the bit you're quoting.

When he has Farfrae in his power, Henchard suddenly stops himself from killing him and moves away in sadness. Farfrae leaves, rejecting his former friend without another word: "Farfrae regarded him in silence; then went to the hatch and descended through it." (Chapter 38)

Just stick it in as part of your ordinary paragraph.

Sometimes You'll Need Two Sets Of Speech Marks

Speech marks aren't just used for quotations. They're also used when characters speak in novels. It starts to get really confusing when there's a character speaking in the bit you want to quote.

1) You need double speech marks at the start of the quotation.

2) Every time a character speaks, put what they say in single speech marks.

" 'Now, look here my man,' said Mr Jaggers, advancing a step, and pointing to the door. 'Get out of this office. I'll have no feelings here. Get out.' " <u>Great Expectations</u>, Vol. 3, Chapter 51.

Out!

3) Then you've got to put double speech marks at the end of the whole thing.

Speech Marks — because German money talks...

Learn this now — you need speech marks for quoting novels, essays, articles and short quotations.

SECTION SIX — QUOTING & EXAMPLES

Quoting From Poems & Plays

QUOTING PLAYS AND POEMS

Here's where you can make a real mess. Your essay could end up looking like a dog's dinner, unless you take the time now to learn these simple rules for quoting from poems and plays.

This Is How To Quote From A Poem

Leave a space between the bit you're quoting and the paragraphs before and after. Don't use speech marks with the quotation.

> There is a strange feeling of being in a prison:
>
> In every voice, in every ban,
> The mind-forged manacles I hear.
>   ("London", lines 7-8; William Blake)
>
> This feeling is created in people's minds, which forge the chains or "manacles" of the prison.

You must keep each line exactly the same as the original.

Put the title of the poem in speech marks.

Give the line numbers.

Don't forget — short quotations like this always have speech marks.

I keep getting a funny feeling like I'm in a prison...

Never quote more than three lines of a poem. You only need to give the relevant bit.

And This Is How To Quote From Plays

You've got to put long quotations in a separate paragraph, the same as poem quotations.

> Lady Bracknell: Where did the charitable gentleman who had a first-class ticket for this seaside resort find you?
> Jack (gravely): In a hand-bag.
>   (The Importance Of Being Earnest, Act One; Oscar Wilde)

Give the characters' names and the stage directions.

You must give the title and act for the quotation too.

Be careful though — some plays are written in poetry.

The last word of each line should be the same as in the original.

> Antony: Friends, Romans, countrymen, lend me your ears.
>   I come to bury Caesar, not to praise him.
>   (Julius Caesar, Act III, scene ii; William Shakespeare)

If you can, give the scene number as well as the act.

SECTION SIX — QUOTING & EXAMPLES

Other Literature Examples

PARAPHRASE & CONTEXT EXAMPLES

Quoting isn't the only kind of groovy example you can stick in your literature essays.

Write About Bits Of The Book In Your Own Words

This lets you make quick points when you haven't got time to quote loads of stuff.

> In the opening chapter of Great Expectations, Dickens sets the scene and straightaway moves into the story of the escaped convict. Immediately we feel sorry for Pip, because he is very young and he is terrified of the convict's threats.

But watch out — you can only do this if you put exactly where the bit comes from in the book.

Don't try this unless you know the book well.

You've Got To Use Background Information Too

1) Make sure you learn the dates of all the books you study.

> Steinbeck wrote Of Mice and Men in 1937, when the effects of the Great Depression were still being felt.

2) If it's relevant, you must be able to give a little bit of historical background to books.

That's what I call 'background' information!

Groan

> Orwell's 1984 was published in 1949, when people remembered the horrors of Nazi Germany and the Second World War, and there was still a threat from the Communist USSR. This was one reason why it had such an impact — people thought that an all-powerful government like the one in the novel could really exist.

3) Only give background information when it's relevant to the essay you're writing.

> What do you think is the most important theme in The Crucible?
> You might like to think about.
> - the events leading up to the final scene
> - persecution and jealousy in Salem
> - the religious and historical background to the play.

4) This time the question tells you to write about background information in your essay.

A librarian's love-life — dating books, maybe...

Phew. Lots of things to learn here. Make sure you learn all this quoting and background stuff now.

SECTION SIX — QUOTING & EXAMPLES

Examples in English Essays

GIVING EXAMPLES FOR ENGLISH

Examples aren't just for literature essays — you've got to use them in your English essays too.

You Need Examples for English Essays

1) Some questions actually tell you to give examples.

> Write an article for a teenage magazine in which you **argue** the case for more help to be given for the homeless. You should:
> - outline the present situation
> - give examples of the sort of people affected by homelessness
> - suggest what more can be done.

2) Look out for sneaky questions that want examples even though they don't directly say so.

> Many families have their own particular traditions. These may be to do with how they celebrate holidays, religious festivals or particular times of the year. Write about your family traditions and explain their importance to you.

3) This wants you to go through each tradition and give examples of the things you do and why they're important.

Some English Essays Need Quotations Too

Watch out for media and comprehension questions.
You must remember to quote from the extracts they give you to back up your points.

> Refer to the extract: What part did Max play in the events described? How does he make his account entertaining for his readers?

Don't worry — just follow the same rules as for literature essays.
Your quotations must be relevant to the points of your answer.

> Write about the medicine man and the young doctor. You should include:
> - what they do
> - how they are different
> - how the writers use words to describe them.

You'll need quotations to back up your points for each bit of this question.

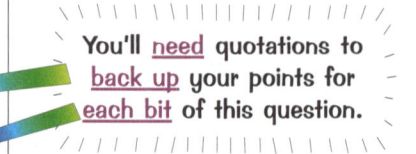

Cloning old boyfriends — give me an ex-sample...

Every essay you write needs examples. Sometimes the question even tells you what examples you need. That's an absolute gift for picking up marks — as long as you make sure you stick them in.

SECTION SIX — QUOTING & EXAMPLES

Finding English Examples

SOURCES FOR ENGLISH EXAMPLES

The trouble with English essays is you don't have anywhere obvious to find examples. With literature essays it's simple because you're writing about a specific book. Here are a few places you can definitely find examples — as long as they're relevant.

How To Find Examples For An English Essay

> A friend has written you a letter saying she/he is thinking of leaving home and asking for your advice. Write a reply trying to persuade her/him not to leave home.

Let me down!

① Personal Experience

Don't be afraid to use anything that's happened in your life which is relevant.

> Three years ago, my brother decided to leave home. He'd had enough of my Mum's strict rules. After four months, he had run out of money and couldn't find a job.

② Books, Films Or Television

Sounds dead obvious, maybe, but these are great places for you to find examples.

> In a recent Channel 6 documentary called "Leaving Home", several homeless people were interviewed. Many of them had left well-off, middle-class homes during their teens, but found themselves living on the streets.

③ Statistics

Statistics mean number facts — they show that you've done your research.

> According to a recent survey, only 16% of people consider themselves to be happy with their lives.

④ Historical Background Stuff

> In the 18th and 19th Centuries, young women were not allowed to leave home until they got married. At least it isn't that bad nowadays.

16% of Harold was a little green monster.

A wallet glued to Alfred — a purse-on-Al experience...

Never make your examples up — especially statistics or quotations. If they spot it you're done for.

SECTION SIX — QUOTING & EXAMPLES

Revision Summary

This is pretty easy stuff. There are a few different things you have to know about how to give examples, but none of it's hard. And if you can answer all of these questions, then you've got it sorted. So you'd better make sure you can.

1) What are the two ways of backing up points in your essays?
2) What's really important about any words you use from a book or poem?
3) Why shouldn't you write essay plans in your set books before the exam?
4) What should you do instead?
5) What are the rules about adding or taking words away from quotations?
6) What should you do if the spelling in the original is wrong?
7) What information do you need to give the first time you quote from a book in your essay?
8) What information do you need to give the next time you quote from the same book?
9) What information do you need for quoting from a different book by the same author?
10) What information do you need to give for quoting a different book by a different author?
11) Do you need speech marks with short quotations?
12) When do you need two sets of speech marks?
13) How do you tell them apart if there are two sets of speech marks?
14) How do you give a three line quotation from a poem?
15) What do you need for a short (a few words long) quotation from a poem?
16) How do you give a quotation from a play?
17) How do you give a quotation from a play that's written in poetry?
18) What do you have to do if you write about part of a book in your own words?
19) What are the four places it's easy to find examples for English essays from?

SECTION SIX — QUOTING & EXAMPLES

SECTION SEVEN — COMPARING

How To Compare

THE BASICS OF COMPARING THINGS

You can guarantee it — there are always comparing questions in English and English Literature. It's one of those things examiners love — so make sure you learn this section carefully.

Comparing = Finding Similarities And Differences

Comparing is all about looking at two or more things together.

Similarities and differences.

Compare these two articles. You should consider:
– the language used
– the ideas they contain
– how the material is presented

You've got to describe the similarities and differences between the articles for each of these points.

Don't Just Write About One Thing And Then The Other

This is the big mistake people make with comparisons. The whole point of the question is that you write about both things together. It's about making links between them.

① – the language used

You need to say whether the language is similar or different in the two articles, along with examples to prove your point.

② – the ideas they contain

Here you need to look at the ideas in both articles. You're trying to make links between ideas that are similar and ideas that are different.

③ – how the material is presented

You have to write about the layout of the two articles for this bit of the question — see Section Eleven for more about this.

ALWAYS give examples.

You must make your comparisons clear — give the similarities and differences, and try to explain why the two things are similar or different.

Designing golf courses — that's making links...

Comparing things can be a real problem — if you don't get the method right. You've got to write about both of the things at the same time — looking at what they have in common, and what they don't. As long as you write about the similarities and differences when you answer the question, you'll be absolutely fine. If you can write good comparing essays, you'll definitely score good marks.

Comparing Two Poems

How To Compare Two Poems

Most of the comparing you'll have to do will be between articles or poems — but don't worry, the method is the same whatever you're comparing.

First Look At What The Question's Asking

This question's asking you how two poems make you feel — which bits from the poems bring the war to life for you.

> How have the conditions of soldiers at war been made real to you in two of the poems from this selection?

It could be the images, the ideas or the language of the poems — any of these things that give you a sense of what soldiers at war go through.

My beautiful creation! I made you live!

Remember — you've got to write about two poems. The best way to make sure you do is to compare them.

Watch Out — This Question Doesn't Say Compare

1) This question doesn't use the word "compare". In fact, you might think it isn't a comparing question at all.
2) Be careful though — the question asks you to look at two poems in detail, and you've only got a short time to fit both of them in.
3) Don't write about one poem and then the other — that's boring.
4) The quickest and clearest way to write about both of them together is by comparing how they make the conditions real.
5) That'll show the examiners that you've understood the poems and that you've understood the question — which definitely means good marks.

It's comparing in disguise.

Spotting comparing questions is easy — if it asks about more than one piece of writing, it's a comparing question.

You Need Good Notes On Each Poem

Now you need to find the bits that bring the war to life in each poem. Read each one in turn and scribble some quick notes.

"Attack" by Siegfried Sassoon
- the start is a general description of battlefield dawn
- landscape: it describes whole ridge - then the tanks
- how the soldiers are weighed down by equipment
- bristling fire of the guns and the grey muttering fear
- the soldiers' furtive eyes and the mud as they go over the top - a desperate prayer to make it stop

Gustav just loved to make quick notes.

Jot down anything you notice — even if it seems really obvious.

Section Seven — Comparing

More On Comparing Two Poems

GETTING YOUR PLANNING MATERIAL

This is the stuff you'll really need to know — how to find things to write about.

Keep Your Notes Clear And Brief

Jot down the main things about the conditions of the soldiers in the other poem.

> "Break of Day in the Trenches" by Isaac Rosenberg
> - darkness changes to day   - not general but specific
> - A soldier sees a rat in the trench...
> - the poem's narrator is actually there himself
>   funny image of the rat crossing between the two sides like a traitor
> - The soldiers are described as strong- but the rat sees their fear
> - Poppies in men's veins at the end is an image of the blood of the dead

This is a big point — it's a very obvious thing, but it's still worth lots of marks if you write about it.

You need to think about what happens and why it happens — why the poet is telling you this.

Make A List Of Similarities And Differences...

Now you need to work out the links between the two poems. You've got to find ideas, images and bits of language in the two poems that you can write about together.

Think how they're linked. Poem 1 — Poem 2

Find the obvious similarities — and short quotations to back them up.

Similarities	Differences
- fear of soldiers - "masked with fear" ("Attack") - "heart aghast" ("B. of D")	-"Attack" starts with gen. description; "B. of Day" with one person in the trench...

This is an obvious difference — but only if you think about it.

...And Then Make Your Plan

Start with your main point — the soldiers' fear in the trenches.

> 1. Both poems are about the soldiers' fear - "Attack" shows fear of going over top . "Break of Day." shows fear in the trenches - "shrieking iron" etc.
> 2. "Attack" is about the whole situation - it only gets personal at the end - with the prayer to "make it stop" BUT "B. of Day." is all in the voice of a soldier throughout - It shows how one soldier's mind works...

This is the main difference — the two poems show the war from different points of view, so they give different ideas.

Comparisons are odious — must be why I hate them...

It's true. You've got to state the blindingly obvious — if you don't, you'll lose lots of valuable marks.

SECTION SEVEN — COMPARING

How To Write A Comparison — Writing Your Comparisons

Once you've done the planning, you've got to do the actual writing. This is where most people go wrong with comparisons — they don't write about the two things together. Read this lot carefully.

Keep The Poems Linked Together

1) Start by making a clear point about something both poems make you feel.

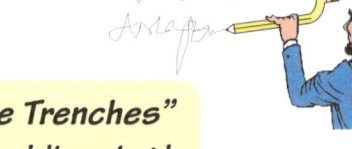

> "Attack" by Siegfried Sassoon and "Break of Day in the Trenches" by Isaac Rosenberg give a clear sense of what it was like for soldiers in the First World War. Both poems show the fear of soldiers in battle.

2) Make sure you're giving a proper answer to the question too.

3) Now you can give a brief description of what the two poems are about.

4) You've got to bring your writing to life. Try to use interesting phrases like this.

> Sassoon's poem is about a dawn attack and the horrible feeling of "going over the top", while Rosenberg's is about dawn in the trenches when the enemy are bombarding it with "shrieking iron and flame".

5) This is also showing some of the similarities and differences between the poems.

Quote Examples And Then Link Them

6) Remember to give some examples from each poem, showing how it describes the soldiers and their feelings.

> In Sassoon's poem, there is a clear description of the soldiers before an attack. He describes them just before they go over the top as, "Lines of grey, muttering faces, masked with fear." Then, he gives an even stronger image of their suffering:
>
> > And hope, with furtive eyes and grappling fists,
> > Flounders in mud.
>
> He is describing hope like a soldier stuck in the mud. This is a clever image of how pointless the war feels for the soldiers on the ground.

Give egg-samples.

7) Don't forget to give accurate quotations...

8) ...and remember to explain them clearly.

9) Sentences like this show the examiners you're writing about both poems together — that means serious marks.

> Rosenberg's poem is very different. It doesn't give a general picture, but starts off with the poet noticing a rat in the trench...

SECTION SEVEN — COMPARING

More About Writing Comparisons

MORE ON WRITING COMPARISONS

Phew — this is getting really tricky now. It's all about how well you write — how clear you are in making your points and showing what the poems have made you feel.

Make Sure You Get The Main Points Into Your Answer

You've got to get the big points from your plan into your answer. One of them was that Rosenberg's poem is much more personal than Sassoon's.

> This is much more personal than "Attack", which gives a general idea. Instead Rosenberg takes us into the mind of a soldier in the trenches, and what he is actually thinking about while the trench is being attacked. Sassoon describes a battle scene more clearly, but he doesn't take you into the soldiers' minds.

You need to explain what the two poems are like — what each one makes you feel.

You Need To Compare The Images In The Poems

Writing about images means picking out the phrases or words that stick in your mind.

Images keep sticking in my mind...

> Some of the images used in both poems are very similar. "Attack" talks about the "scarred slope", while "Break of Day in the Trenches" talks about the "torn fields of France". These images give an idea of what the landscape looked like — it looked like it was scarred and wounded just like the soldiers.

You have to explain what kind of picture they give you — why they stick in your mind.

Your Writing Must Be Interesting And Clear

Examiners always give good marks to people who write clearly and use interesting phrases.

These phrases are really interesting, but they also explain clearly what the last bit of the poem is like.

> The final idea in Sassoon's poem is a desperate prayer — "Oh Jesus, make it stop!" Suddenly the poem becomes very personal. All of the description that went before is summed up in this short cry of despair.

Jellyfish in space — clear and interesting.

You've got to tell the examiners what the poems are like as clearly as if they've never read them.

Let's swap poems — I need a change of image...

This is incredibly important. You've got to keep in mind these questions are marked on how well you answer the question, and how well you write — whether you use interesting words and tell the examiners clearly what the poems are like, as if they've never actually read them.

SECTION SEVEN — COMPARING

Comparing Three Or Four Things

COMPARISONS WITH THREE OR MORE

Some questions ask you to compare three or four things. No problem — just use the same method as you do for two.

Lots Of Poetry Questions Ask For Three Or Four Poems

> Compare three or four poems from this selection, showing how poets use events in their own lives to explore what writing is about.

Just Use The Same Method For Comparing Them

Whatever you do, don't panic — the examiners only want to see if you really know how to compare things.

> Compare three or four poems from the selection which deal with painful experiences. You should write about:
> – the nature of the experiences, and how these are dealt with
> – how the poets get their feelings across
> – differences between the poems

You need to choose three or four poems, and look for these things. Then jot down a list of similarities and differences, make your final plan and write your answer.

Use the same tricks as when you compare just two.

You must write about all three or four poems together, and talk about similarities and differences.

Don't Confuse The Different Poems

1) Sometimes people don't make it clear which poem they're writing about.

2) This is really confusing for the examiners — you'll lose marks for being unclear.

3) As long as you have a list of similarities and differences, and a clear plan, you'll be fine.

4) Always put clearly which poem you're writing about, even if it's got a long name. This is especially important when you're writing about poems by the same author.

> "Ode on a Grecian Urn" is different from "Ode to Autumn" in several ways...

5) Both of these poems are by Keats, so you couldn't put: Keats' poem is different from the other one...

The life of Keats — all odes lead to Rome...

This method might look like a lot of work, but it's the easiest way to sort out all the facts you need. You've got to keep it all organised if you're writing about three or four poems together. The main thing is, don't confuse which bits come from which poem. As long as you keep the similarities and differences in mind, you'll be fine. And always remember to answer the question clearly.

SECTION SEVEN — COMPARING

Common Comparison Topics

SOME POPULAR QUESTION TOPICS

The best bit about comparisons is that you always get asked questions about the same kind of thing.

You'll Be Asked To Compare Ideas and Themes

Compare the way Wordsworth and R. S. Thomas write about childhood.
Write about any three poems, including at least one by each poet, and say:
- what the poet tells us about childhood
- why the poet thinks childhood is important
- how the poets use language to get their ideas across

You'll Also Be Asked To Compare The Language

Watch out — this question is only asking for the differences.

Choose three of four poems from this group.
What differences in the use of language do you notice?
You should write about:
- language which tells you about background and character
- language which is formal and informal
- words which are chosen for a particular effect

Sometimes You've Got To Compare How Two Poets Write

Compare the way Keats and Frost write about nature.
Choose two or three poems, at least one by each poet, and say:
- what the poem has to say about nature
- how the poet gets his ideas about nature across
- which poem you liked best and why

One Final Tip:

When you compare poems, the instructions may say you must write about poems from before the 20th century and poems from the 20th century. Always do exactly what the instructions say.

Land's End rubbish dump — another final tip...

These beauties are the sort of comparison questions you'll be asked in exams and coursework. They can ask you to compare themes, language and the way the poets write. Don't forget the Final Tip.

SECTION SEVEN — COMPARING

Revision Summary

Comparing questions can sound really nasty, but they're only a headache if you don't plan them well. If you just follow a few basic rules, you'll be fine. Make your notes, list as many similarities and differences as you can find, then plan your essay. Then all you've got to do is write it — but if you've done the other bits properly the writing will be dead easy. Have a go at these questions to make sure you know what to do. Try to answer them without looking back through the section — though that might take a few attempts...

1) What does comparing really mean?
2) What's the biggest mistake people make with comparisons?
3) Why do you need to make your comparisons clear?
4) What two kinds of text usually turn up in comparing questions?
5) What should you look at first when you're comparing?
6) Why do you need to write comparisons for some questions, when they don't use the word "compare" in the title?
7) Why do you need to jot down obvious things when you're making notes?
8) Why do you need to make a list of similarities and differences to help you plan your answer?
9) What kind of point should you start your plan with?
10) Where do most people go wrong with comparisons, and why?
11) How should you start your actual answer?
12) Should you: a) give examples from the poems to back up the points you make, or b) write an essay about your socks?
13) What's a good way to bring your writing to life?
14) What do you need to remember about any quotations you use?
15) How can you explain what two poems are like in your answer?
16) How should you write about the images in the poems?
17) What things do the examiners give good marks for in your writing style?
18) Why is it a good idea to assume the examiners have never read the poems?
19) Do you still use the same basic method when you're asked to compare three or four poems?
20) Why can you lose marks if you don't make clear which poem you're writing about?
21) How should you make it clear which poem you're writing about?
22) What three different things could you be asked to compare?
23) Compare two articles about the same subject from any newspaper or magazine. Try to use the skills from this section to help you plan and write your answer. It should be at least one page long.

That one's heavier, this one's cuter...

'Compearing.'

SECTION EIGHT — INFORMATION WRITING

Describing
How To Write Descriptions

Describing something means saying what it is and what it's like. Sounds obvious, I know, but it's one of those skills that can make a big difference to all your writing... and win you extra marks.

Keep Your Describing Interesting

Lots of questions ask you to describe things. Like this one:

> Journeys can be exciting, boring or a mixture of both.
> **Describe** a journey you have made, so that the reader can imagine it clearly.

Watch out — there isn't a proper question to answer here. The only way to do well is to make your description as interesting to read as possible.

You Need To Be Careful How You Use Words

① Don't use the same words all the time — it's seriously dull to read.

> It was a fascinating train trip, through miles of fascinating desert. I met lots of fascinating people too...

= BORING

You need to find different words to describe everything — you're trying to help the reader imagine what the journey was like.

> It was a fascinating train trip, through miles of empty desert. I met lots of entertaining people too...

Exciting!

This is much better. It's a lot more exciting to read.

② Don't use too many vague describing words, like interesting or beautiful.
Don't use them on their own — always add extra information to back them up.

> The desert was beautiful because it was so open and bare.

If you back them up, you'll make your description clearer to understand.

> The old man was interesting to talk to, because he was one of the workers who had built the railway forty years ago.

Never use the word "nice" — it doesn't really mean anything.
Think of some other word to use instead.

A drilling machine — that's a boring description...

These tips may look pretty simple, but people always forget them. Describing is much more difficult than you think. Don't keep using the same words and watch out for those vague words.

More On Writing Descriptions
More On Describing

Apart from using different words and explaining vague terms, there are a few other things you can do to improve your marks for describing questions.

Try Using Images To Bring Your Writing To Life

Images are word pictures — they make your writing more fun.

1) You can give a clear picture by saying what something is like.

   The coach lurched forward like a dog chasing a stick.

2) You can also compare things using as — "as fat as", "as ugly as" etc.

   The rooster on her lap was as big as a Christmas turkey.

3) You can write that something actually is something else.

   The sandstorm turned the sky to chocolate.

   The sky isn't really chocolate, it's like chocolate. This is just a dramatic way of saying it.

Avoid Using Clichés

Clichés are phrases or images that have been used so often they've become boring.

He is as hard as nails.   *Football is a game of two halves.*

You win some, you lose some.   *It was as dead as a dodo.*

Try not to use them in your descriptions — you'll lose marks for being dull.

Don't Use Slang Or Jargon Words

1) Slang is the sort of language you use out of school with your mates. Don't use it in your descriptions — the examiners won't know what you mean.

2) Jargon is any sort of technical terms that most people wouldn't understand, like sports terms or police terms from TV. Don't use them unless you explain what they mean.

   It's first and goal from the seven-yard line. = American football jargon.

Clichés — they're as dull as ditchwater...

Be careful with descriptions — don't use clichés, slang or jargon — but try to give clear images.

SECTION EIGHT — INFORMATION WRITING

Informing

INFORMING QUESTIONS

Informing means telling people information — giving them the facts. The key to answering informing questions is making absolutely certain you get your facts across clearly.

Remember — Informing Means Giving The Facts

These questions can be a real gift — you can pick up easy marks for your answer.

> People often enjoy reading about the interests and hobbies of others. Choose something you are interested in and know a lot about. Write about this in a way which will **inform** other people.

This one's asking you to give facts about something you like and know about — talk about giving away marks.

Keep Your Answer Simple

1) You've got to assume that the examiners know absolutely nothing about your hobby — even if it's football.

> For the last five years, I have played football for a Sunday League team. I play in goal, which means I am allowed to use my hands to touch the ball, but only inside a certain area of the field.

2) This is all obvious stuff — that's the point.
   The examiners just want to see how well you can tell them about it.

3) Don't leave anything out because you think the examiners must know it — maybe they don't.

> The offside rule is something that always confuses people. In fact, it isn't as difficult as people make it out to be. A player is offside when...

4) There are loads of lovely marks to be won here — as long as you give plenty of information as clearly as you can.

5) Don't forget that you're writing about something you enjoy — you've got to make it sound exciting.

> The best thing about football is the feeling you get when you've just made a good save. You feel proud and relieved but you know you've still got to concentrate, because the rest of team is relying on you to do your job. You feel under pressure, but in a good way.

What a footballer — he's definitely in-form...

Informing questions are a chance to pick up easy marks — but only if you go through the basics. Don't assume the examiners know anything — tell them about the topic in as much detail as you can.

SECTION EIGHT — INFORMATION WRITING

How To Write An Explanation — Explaining

Here's the last of these irritating question terms. Explaining means telling people what, how or why something happens or happened. Don't worry — it isn't as hard as it sounds.

You've Got To Think About The Question

This is a typical "explaining" question — it asks you to choose a specific thing and explain it.

> Choose an event from your past that has particular significance for you. **Explain** what happened and your feelings about it.

You need to write about two different things here — what happened and how you felt about it.

You need to answer both parts of the question together. Don't stick on a bit about your feelings right at the end.

Explaining What Happened Is Just Telling A Story

1) All you have to do is give the facts — how, what and why.

> Three years ago, my parents decided to go on holiday without taking my brother and me. They wanted our aunt to come and look after us, but she was ill. After a long argument, they finally decided to let us stay behind and look after ourselves. That was when the trouble started...

2) Make sure you don't leave anything important out.

3) Start writing about your feelings at the beginning of your answer too.

I think I've left something important out...

> At first I was excited. No parents to boss us around! We could even have a party, and they would never have to know. Then I started to feel a little nervous. What if there was some sort of problem? We would have to sort it out ourselves...

4) You're trying to help the examiners understand how what happened affected you — what you thought, what you said, whether it made you happy, sad or worried.

Try to say why you had the feelings you did, as well as what they were.

An average-looker after a facelift — ex-plain...

How, what and why — that's what explaining is all about. It's one of the most annoyingly dull things you have to do in English, but you can actually pick up some valuable marks if you do it well.

More On Explaining

MORE ON EXPLAINING QUESTIONS

Some explaining questions <u>aren't</u> like stories at all. They're about things that <u>happen regularly</u>.

Remember To Say How, What And Why

Here's a question is asking you about things that <u>happen regularly</u> in your family.

> Many families have their own particular traditions. These may be to do with how they celebrate holidays, religious festivals or particular times of the year. Write about your family traditions and **explain** their importance to you.

<u>This bit</u> means you've got to write about <u>what</u> you do...

...and this bit's asking you <u>why</u> you do these things, and <u>what they mean</u> to your family.

You Need To Make It Clear And Interesting

1) Try to make your answer <u>interesting</u> for the examiners to read — give lots of <u>details</u> and keep your explanation <u>clear</u> to follow.

2) Use plenty of <u>different words</u> rather than the same ones all the time.

3) Don't worry if it <u>isn't</u> the most amazingly thrilling piece of writing in the world — as long as you've done <u>what the question asked</u> and explained things <u>clearly</u>, you'll pick up <u>marks</u>.

4) If you really <u>can't</u> think of anything interesting to write about, then <u>don't</u> answer a question like this. Find one that you <u>can</u> answer in an interesting way.

> If your writing is <u>interesting</u>, you'll pick up <u>more marks</u>.
> If your writing is <u>boring</u> or <u>sounds bored</u>, you <u>won't</u>.

Don't Make Things Up

When you answer questions like this, it's <u>tempting</u> to <u>make things up</u> that sound <u>more interesting</u>.

NO! → *Every 27th of January, my family celebrates Wibble Day. Wibble Day is an ancient winter festival where everyone has to dress up in green clothes and paint their faces with blue cheese...*

<u>Never</u> make things up — it may be funny <u>to you</u>, but the examiners <u>won't</u> be impressed, and you'll <u>lose important marks</u> for doing it.

There's no excuse — you have to explain yourself...

Explaining questions are about being <u>clear</u> — but they're also about writing in an <u>interesting way</u>. You need to use <u>different words</u> and give plenty of <u>detail</u> to do well. <u>Boring writing</u> means <u>low marks</u>.

SECTION EIGHT — INFORMATION WRITING

Revision Summary

Nice and short — a five page section. But you still need to know all the stuff in it, not just vaguely let your eyes drift over it. Really KNOW it. The best way to make sure you do know it all is to answer these questions. If there are some you can't do, look back to find the answers. Then try them again. And again. And again. Until you can answer them in your sleep. Then you'll be able to breeze through your exam. Sounds good to me.

1) Why shouldn't you use the same words all the time?
2) What's wrong with words like "interesting" or "beautiful"?
3) Is the word "nice" a good one to use?
4) What are images?
5) Why should you use images?
6) Give an example of an image using "like".
7) Give an example of an image using "as".
8) Give an example of an image where something actually "is" something else.
9) What are clichés?
10) Why shouldn't you use them in your writing?
11) What is slang?
12) Why shouldn't you use it in your writing?
13) What is jargon?
14) Why shouldn't you use it in your writing?
15) What do you have to assume that the examiners know?
16) How do you answer if the question asks you to explain two things?
17) If the question asks you to explain your feelings, what should you say apart from what they were?

"We write 'in-formation'."

SECTION EIGHT — INFORMATION WRITING

SECTION NINE — PERSUADING

Persuading
How To Write Persuasively

Persuading means making someone accept your point of view. It's more forceful than "arguing a case" (see p.47). You're trying to show that your opinion is right and any other opinion is wrong.

You've Got To Make People Believe You're Right

This is the sort of question you've got to answer.

> Write a letter to the RSPCA to **persuade** them to accept you as a volunteer. You should:
> - remember to set out your answer as a letter
> - write about the sort of things you are able to do
> - persuade the RSPCA that you would be a suitable volunteer

You need to do two things — put your answer in the right style, and make the RSPCA believe that you're right for the job.

Imagine You're Trying To Change Their Minds

The best way to persuade people is to think up all the arguments against your opinion.

Reasons RSPCA wouldn't accept me
— too young - lack of experience
— not enough time to spend
— what could I actually do to help?

The RSPCA wouldn't accept me because I keep eating things...

Then you've got to work out how to prove them wrong.

— too young - but parents say it's OK
— lack of experience - but eager to learn & love animals
— no time - can arrange to do it on weekends & after school
— what could I do? - willing to do anything to help

Come on punk, make my day!

You Need To Be Positive

If you sound positive and certain that you're right, people are much more likely to believe you.

I am exactly the sort of person you're looking for. ← This is great — it's really positive.

NO! This is terrible. → Perhaps I might be alright at doing this after a while.

Paddling in wallets — that's purse-wading...

Wake up — I know it's tempting to doze off when you're reading this stuff, but it's actually pretty darn important. Learning about persuading isn't just useful for persuading questions — it'll improve the way you write essays too, and that means more marks. It's worth staying awake for.

PERSUASIVE LANGUAGE

Some Persuading Tricks

Persuading is all about making people believe you. Here are a few sneaky tricks you can practise to help you improve your persuading skills — and pick up more marks for your work.

Persuading Is Like Selling A Product

You've got to sell your point of view to the examiners — as if it's the best possible answer.

> Write a letter in which you try to **persuade** your school governors to get rid of school uniforms.

Frankly, this new uniform is ridiculous.

You Can Exaggerate To Stress Key Points

1) Exaggerating means making something out to be more than it really is.

   > School uniforms are a form of torture for most of us.

2) You don't really mean it's a torture — it's just an over-the-top way to stress your point.

3) You're making your points sound a lot more impressive than they really are.

   > The biggest reason why people hate this place is the uniform. Everyone is sick of those pink jumpers.

4) Don't just make things up though — even though you're exaggerating, you've still got to back up the things you're saying with real, sensible examples.

Use Exaggeration to Criticise The Opposite Opinion

1) You can use exaggerated language to criticise the opposite opinion to your own.

   > The idea that the uniforms give us a sense of identity is a complete fantasy.

Well, at least this uniform's cheap...

2) You don't literally mean the idea is a fantasy — it's an over-the-top image (see P.70).

3) Make sure you give clear, proper reasons to back up your opinion as well.

   > In fact, the uniform is expensive, uncomfortable and embarrassing to wear, as most students will tell you.

Don't be rude — exaggerating doesn't mean you can start writing abuse. You'll lose marks if you do — and get yourself into a lot of trouble.

I've told you a million times — stop exaggerating...

Exaggerating is about making things sound more impressive than they really are, but don't be rude.

SECTION NINE — PERSUADING

More On Persuading

MORE PERSUASIVE LANGUAGE

The <u>way</u> you write for people can <u>affect</u> whether or not they <u>believe</u> you — you need to strike a balance between being <u>polite</u> and <u>formal</u> and getting them <u>on your side</u>.

Keep Your Writing Polite

This is <u>very important</u> when you're writing about people with the <u>opposite opinion</u> to yours.

I think we should wear whatever we want.

> Many people say school uniforms are a necessary part of the education system. They are entitled to that opinion, but I believe it is totally wrong.

You should criticise their <u>opinions only</u>. <u>Don't</u> criticise them <u>personally</u> — you'll <u>lose marks</u> for being rude.

Keep Any Negative Points Impersonal

1) If you're going to <u>criticise</u> an <u>opinion</u>, do it <u>without</u> writing about the <u>people</u> who think it.

NO! → A lot of people think school uniforms make everyone equal. They are wrong...

2) Watch it — this sounds like a <u>personal attack</u>. It makes you sound <u>angry</u>, which will put the examiners' backs up. It <u>won't</u> help you persuade <u>anyone</u>.

3) This is <u>much better</u> — you're criticising the <u>opinion</u>, not the <u>people</u>.

> It is often said that school uniforms make everyone equal. This isn't true...

But Make Your Positive Points Personal

You need to make the readers <u>feel</u> that you're all on the <u>same side</u>.

I reckon I'm individual...

> <u>We</u> all believe that individuality is important.

This "<u>we</u>" makes it sound like your readers <u>agree</u> with you <u>already</u>.

You can also use "<u>you</u>" to talk <u>directly</u> to your readers, especially if you're trying to <u>persuade</u> them to <u>do</u> something.

> <u>You</u> have a chance to prove that today by getting rid of uniforms.

It's as if you're trying to <u>persuade</u> them <u>personally</u>.

A charming Teletubby lamp — Po-light...

Phew — this <u>positive</u> and <u>negative</u> lark sounds pretty tricky. All it means is you need to stay <u>polite</u> when you make any <u>bad points</u> about the <u>opposite view</u> to yours — and <u>don't</u> attack <u>people</u>.

SECTION NINE — PERSUADING

Three Useful Tricks

We're nearly finished with persuading — but here are a few more **useful tricks** to keep handy when you're answering a **persuading** question.

Try To Use "We" And "Us" When You Can

This goes back to the bit on P.77 about using **personal** language when you're making **positive points**.

<u>We</u> have all heard that...   <u>Our</u> future depends on...

The problem <u>we</u> face is...   This affects <u>us</u> all...

See if you can use **phrases like these** to help your argument sound **more convincing**.

You Should Also Use Questions To Make Your Points

1) It's a brilliant **trick** that **writers** and **politicians** use all the time.

   Is this sort of thing acceptable in our society?

2) You're leaving it to the **readers** to give the answer, **instead** of saying it yourself — it's a great way of making them **agree with you**.

   Can anyone tell me why the motorway builders are ruining the countryside?

3) You need to use **exaggerated language** like "ruining the countryside". It **tells** the readers what **your opinion** really is, which will make them **think** about it **more carefully**.

Motorways are great for rocket-powered rollerblading.

Improve The Style Of Your Answer With Magic Threes

One of the **easiest** and **most useful** tricks for **emphasising** your points. Instead of just using **one describing word** in a sentence, use **three**.

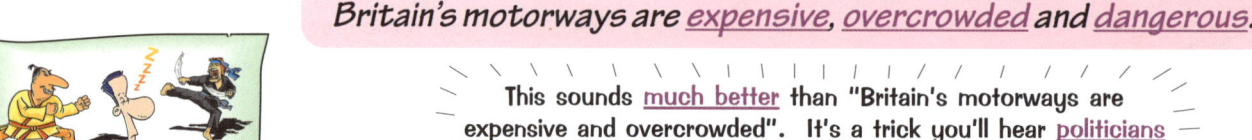

Britain's motorways are expensive, overcrowded and dangerous.

This sounds **much better** than "Britain's motorways are expensive and overcrowded". It's a trick you'll hear **politicians** using in **speeches** — it **stresses** the points you're making.

Heaney's poems are clever, well-written and moving.

You can use it in your **Literature essays** too.

The Good, the Bad and the Dopey
Starring Beano Reevee, Goldie Woopsberg and Demi A. Favour.
Directed by Tintin Quarantino. Filmed in Crumby-gag-o-vision.

A magic three — Gandalf, Merlin & the Wizard of Oz...

Three lovely little tricks to **learn** here. Try to use "**we**" and "**us**" to make your answer **more personal** — and **don't forget** to use **questions** and **magic threes** to **emphasise** the points you're making.

Revision Summary

OK, now it's my turn to persuade you to do these questions: if you do them, your exam will be <u>loads easier</u>. That's what all this boils down to. Go through the questions and answer them. Look up any you can't do, and do them again. Keep doing it until you can answer them all. Relax — for a while. Then come back and check you can still do them.

1) What kind of notes should you make when you have to persuade someone?
2) What do you do with the points in them?
3) When you are writing to persuade, should you sound:
   (a) positive and confident, or *(b)* negative as if you know you haven't got a chance?
4) What's like selling a product?
5) Which bits in your answer are worth exaggerating?
6) Give an example that's bad because it criticises someone personally.
7) What should you criticise instead? Rewrite your example in this way.
8) When you've got negative points and positive points, when should you be personal? When should you be impersonal?
9) Give examples of when it's good to be personal and when it's bad.
10) Give three phrases with "we" and "us" that you could use in your answers.
11) What can you use questions for?
12) Give an example of using a question for this.
13) What are magic threes?
14) Make up a magic three about your favourite TV programme.

"Everyone listen to me or the custard gets it!"

"Sure thing!"

Special Exploding Custard Sticks

"That's <u>persuaded</u> me!"

SECTION NINE — PERSUADING

SECTION TEN — ENDING YOUR WRITING

Ending Your Essays

How To End An Essay

The ending is where <u>essays</u> get <u>really tough</u>.
Make sure you <u>remind</u> the examiners that you've <u>definitely</u> answered the question.

You Need To Time Your Ending Exactly Right

<u>Timing</u> your ending is all about knowing <u>when</u> to finish your essay.
It's especially important in <u>exams</u>. You need to <u>leave</u> enough time to answer <u>all</u> the questions.
You also need to <u>answer</u> them <u>properly</u>, which means you <u>must</u> write a <u>clear ending</u>.

How To Write A Good Ending For Your Essay

① It's your <u>last chance</u> to persuade the examiners, so make your <u>main point</u> again.

② Make sure you <u>answer</u> the question <u>clearly</u>. Your opinion may have <u>changed</u> in the course of your essay.

Always Sum Up Your Main Points At The End

> How important are the witches in *Macbeth*?

You need to <u>show</u> the examiners that the essay's <u>nearly over</u>.
Start your ending by summing up the main points.

> *The witches are important because they start the story off. Their prophecies cause Macbeth to wonder if he could become King. Their prophecies cause him to murder Banquo. Every evil thing he does is a result of what the witches say.*
>
> *They are also the first characters who appear in the play. Everything else that follows is surrounded by an air of mystery and superstition. The witches are strange and terrifying and they give the play its weird, ghostly feeling.*
>
> *As well as starting the action, the witches set the supernatural tone of the play — that is why they are important.*

Make your second <u>final point</u> (if you have one).

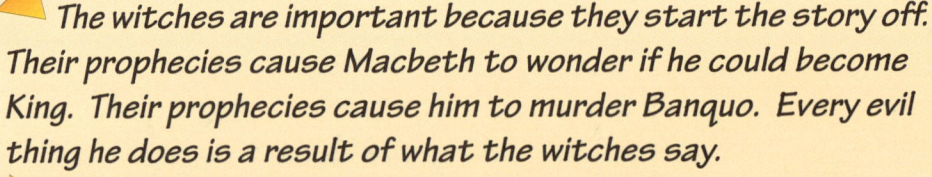

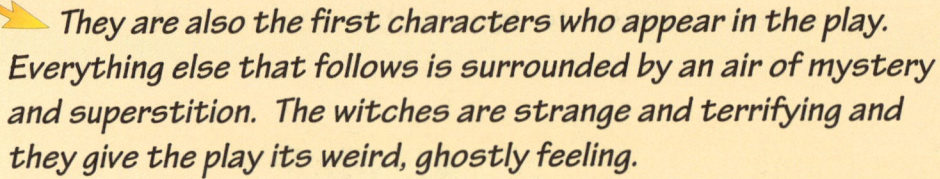

Right at the end, <u>summarise</u> your two final points — the witches <u>start</u> the <u>play's action</u> and they <u>set the tone</u>.

A smiling full stop — now that's a happy ending...

<u>Ending essays</u> is a lot like starting them. It's all about making a few things <u>clear</u> to the examiner. Remember, it's your <u>last chance</u> to show them that your answer fits the question. <u>Learn</u> the <u>two rules</u> for ending an essay. I know this is all pretty dull, but it really will help your <u>marks</u>.

More On Ending Your Essays

WORDING & TIMING YOUR ENDING

This essay-ending stuff sounds very familiar — but you've still got to learn it carefully.
Even if it sounds obvious, it can make a massive difference to your marks.

Try To Use the Exact Question Words Again

> What do you think is the most important theme in *The Crucible*?

It's simple really — try to start your ending with the exact question words.

> The most important theme in *The Crucible* is how every single person has a choice to stand up for what they believe in, whatever the consequences, or to give up their beliefs because of fear.

D'you believe I'm from Mars now?
PFFF!
You're from Mars, you're from Mars, you're from Mars!

This shows the examiners you're coming to the end of the essay, and makes it crystal clear that your essay fits the question.

You Must Leave Enough Time For A Proper Ending

This may sound stupid, but it's surprisingly easy to run out of time in exams.
You've got to leave enough time for answering all the questions you're asked to.
You've also got to leave enough time to finish each essay properly — with a clear ending.

Learn This Checklist

1) Work out how much time you have for each essay before you start.
2) In an exam you need about 40 minutes for each essay, not including planning.
3) Make sure you have a watch to time yourself — and keep checking it.
4) Watch out when you get towards the end of the time for one essay.
5) Make sure you leave yourself five minutes to write an ending for your essay.
6) Do the same thing for each essay you have to write.

> Make sure you leave yourself five minutes to write an ending for each essay.

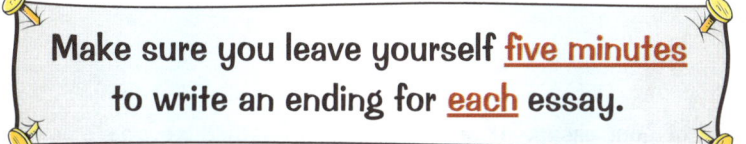

The Crucible — isn't that about snooker...

The end of your essay is a great chance to remind the examiners what you've been saying and bang it home, so that they're completely convinced you've answered the question. Try to use the exact question words to make it even clearer. The main thing is to make sure you leave enough time.

SECTION TEN — ENDING YOUR WRITING

Problems With Ending Essays

ENDING ESSAYS QUICKLY & CLEARLY

Things don't always go to plan with essays. The secret is not to panic.
You'll get marks for ending your essay properly even if the rest of the essay is a mess.

1) If You're Running Out Of Time

If you suddenly realise you're running out of time to finish the essay, stay calm.

> What qualities make "The Lady of Shalott" a memorable poem?

Finish the paragraph that you're writing. Don't just stop in mid-flow.

> All the knights are afraid of the strange appearance of the dead lady, except Lancelot, who doesn't even know that he has caused her death.
> "The Lady of Shalott" is a memorable poem because of the weird, magical atmosphere and the slow, musical rhymes which bring the sad story to life.

Then write a short ending.

If you're really pushed for time, just write one sentence, like this.

Remember you've still got to finish by showing your answer fits the question.

2) If You've Run Out Of Things To Write

This can easily happen too. You can completely run out of anything else to write.
Don't just write any old rubbish — you must stick to the point.

> The only thing Lancelot can say is that she had a "pretty face", and that he hopes God will give her grace.
> This is a memorable poem because the sound of the verse has a hypnotic effect. The Lady is mysterious and her story is tragic, and the whole atmosphere of the poem is strange and mystical.

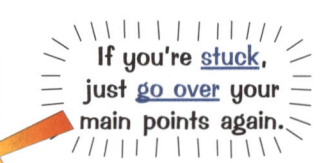

If you're stuck, just go over your main points again.

Some people think I'm quite pretty...

Finish this paragraph like the end of your essay. If you've thought of something else, then carry on. If you haven't, leave this as your ending and move on to the next question.

Phew — more run-outs than English cricket...

Don't panic if you're stuck — go over your main points. If you run out of time, write a short ending.

SECTION TEN — ENDING YOUR WRITING

More Problems With Endings

CHANGING YOUR MIND AT THE END

If you <u>change</u> your <u>point of view</u> it can cause even more trouble.

If You're Still Not Sure About The Answer

1) With some questions you <u>can't decide</u> your point of view straight away.

> Do you feel at all sorry for Farmer Boldwood in <u>*Far From The Madding Crowd*</u>?

2) Instead you need to <u>try</u> to answer it <u>during</u> your essay, so that you can <u>finish up</u> with a <u>clear answer</u>. The big problem comes when you <u>still</u> don't have an answer <u>at the end</u>.

> If you really <u>can't</u> make up your mind, write a final paragraph giving <u>both sides</u> of the case.

Some 'yes' answers. → There are some reasons for feeling sorry for Boldwood. Everything he does stems from his obsession with Bathsheba. He is driven mad by his love and by the cruel way that Troy treats her.

Some 'no' answers. → At the same time, he is a respected farmer and should know better. Instead he neglects his work. Even though he is an intelligent man, he is completely blind to the fact that Bathsheba never really loves him at all. He pressurises her into marriage when she doesn't want it. It is difficult to feel sorry for him then.

4) <u>Make sure</u> you use the <u>exact question wording</u>. Even if you <u>can't</u> choose an answer, the examiners will see you're <u>trying</u> to answer the question.

If You Change Your Mind...

Watch out — you might <u>change your mind</u> about the answer <u>after</u> you've written the whole essay. <u>Don't</u> worry — just <u>carry on</u> with the essay by giving your <u>new opinion</u>.

> At the beginning of this essay, I said that I felt sorry for Farmer Boldwood. Now I'm not so sure. Even though he is in love, his obsession makes him do strange things, and he hurts Bathsheba. Troy hurts Bathsheba because he doesn't love her; Boldwood hurts her because he does. Both of them are cruel to her, and neither of them ever allows her to make her own choices.
> On the surface you can feel sorry for Boldwood, but really he is as much of a villain in the story as Troy.

Here you <u>need</u> to use "I" and be personal.

At the end you <u>also</u> need to explain <u>why</u> you changed your mind.

Changing your mind — swapping brain cells...

If you're <u>unsure</u> of your answer or you've <u>changed</u> your opinion, <u>don't</u> panic. Just explain <u>why</u>.

SECTION TEN — ENDING YOUR WRITING

Ending Letters

ENDING FORMAL & INFORMAL LETTERS

Phew. Ending <u>letters</u> is a lot <u>easier</u>, as long as you learn a few <u>simple rules</u>.

Ending Letters To Friends Or Family

A friend has written you a letter saying she/he is thinking of leaving home and asking for your advice. Write a reply trying to **persuade** her/him not to leave home.

You need to <u>sum up</u> your <u>main points</u> in the <u>last</u> paragraph.

Give it another chance. You know that if you can stay until you've got some qualifications, you'll find it easier to get a job. If you still want to leave then, fair enough. But at least you will have tried.

Take care,

Love,

Mandy

Remember that you're writing to a <u>friend</u> — you <u>don't</u> have to be formal.

You <u>only</u> need to put your <u>first name</u>.

With my degree in Pig Lifting, I'm sure to get a job.

WARNING: most letter questions have a <u>word limit</u>, like "about 200". You need to <u>leave</u> enough words <u>free</u> for your ending. <u>Don't</u> write <u>too much</u>.

Remember — "about 200" means 200-210 is ideal.

Ending Formal Letters

Write a letter to the headteacher in favour of keeping school meals.

<u>Finish</u> your argument with a <u>clear last point</u>.

Unless students are provided with healthy meals at school, their attention spans in class will go down. Thank you very much for your time and attention.

Yours sincerely,

Brian Morgan,
Student Rep.

You must be <u>polite</u> — <u>thank</u> the person for their time.

If you've written the letter with the <u>person's name</u> on it, you must use "Yours sincerely".

Put your <u>full name</u> and who you are.

If you <u>don't know</u> the person's name, <u>address</u> it to "<u>Dear Sir/Madam</u>" and put "<u>Yours faithfully</u>" at the end.

Ending letters — X, Y, and Z...

Time to put <u>everything</u> you know about <u>letters</u> together. <u>Go over</u> this page and p.36 on <u>starting letters</u>.

SECTION TEN — *ENDING YOUR WRITING*

Ending Articles & Reports

ENDING STYLES FOR ARTICLES/REPORTS

It doesn't matter if you're ending or starting them — articles and reports are about one thing. They're all about getting the style right by working out who you're writing for.

The End Of An Article Needs To Make People Think

Don't forget — you're being marked on getting the style right as well as answering the question.

> Write an **article** for your school newspaper about why you think charities for the homeless are important.

I've got a home wherever I am...

Think about the style of a school newspaper article. Keep your sentences short and to the point.

> Homelessness isn't a problem we can ignore, even if we wanted to. There are too many people living on our streets, and the government isn't doing anything about it. Unless we support charities like these, nothing will be done about it. And who knows — the problem might get worse.

Sum up your main points answering the question.

You're arguing a case, so make your writing persuasive.

Your last sentence needs to leave people something to think about.

You Must End A Report With A Clear Conclusion

Reports are like essays but even more formal. You've got to give a clear answer in the right style.

> Write a **report** for the council in which you explain the advantages and disadvantages of each of the three plans for the school road.

Start by summing up the key advantages and disadvantages for each plan.

> To sum up, banning cars on the road during school hours is not practical. There are too many businesses and homes nearby. Reducing the speed limit is a good idea, as long as it is properly enforced. This could definitely be helped by putting in speed bumps as a form of traffic control.
> Even though traffic all around the town would be affected, the second and third plans are worth putting into practice. They could save a child's life.

Based on the whole report, say what you think the council should do and why.

Going back into harbour — that's re-porting...

The secret with reports and articles is to think who you're writing for, and stick to the point.

SECTION TEN — ENDING YOUR WRITING

SUMMING UP DESCRIPTIONS

Ending Descriptions

If they want you to write a <u>description</u>, the question will often be vague.
Description answers are a real pain to <u>start</u> and to <u>finish</u>, so <u>learn</u> this page carefully.

Ending A <u>Description</u> Based On <u>Extracts</u>

Don't forget — your description must be <u>based on</u> what you've <u>read</u> in the extracts.

'Egg tracks.'

> Write about the doctor and the medicine man.
> You should include:
> - what they do
> - how they are different
> - how the writers use words to describe them.

When you've finished the <u>main part</u> of your description, just add a <u>final paragraph</u>. Make sure you put something <u>clear</u> in about <u>each</u> of the things you're <u>told to include</u> in the instructions.

> *The doctor and the medicine man are more similar than they appear at first. Although the doctor uses technology and logic, the medicine man uses experience and practical medicine in a similar way. Both of them are concerned with the patients' well-being in the extracts, and both of them are described as professional, experienced men. In fact, they are actually more similar than different.*

= <u>what</u> they do and <u>how</u> they are different.

= how the writers <u>use words</u> to describe them.

<u>Sum up</u> the <u>similarities</u> and <u>differences</u> between the two healers.

Ending Descriptions — Sum Up <u>What You Think</u>

This is a <u>real stinker</u>. It <u>doesn't</u> ask you a <u>proper question</u>.

> **Describe** a city at night in such a way that it can be easily imagined by your reader.

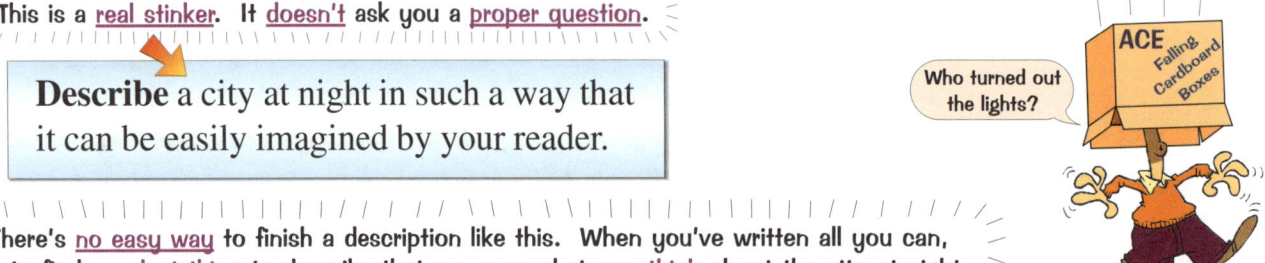

Who turned out the lights?

There's <u>no easy way</u> to finish a description like this. When you've written all you can, try to find <u>one last thing</u> to describe that sums up what <u>you think</u> about the city at night.

> *The city is so dark sometimes that all you can see are the lights, like the stars in the sky. It seems peaceful then, just waiting for the morning when it comes to life again. I love the city at night.*

Finish by giving <u>your opinion</u> — put down what <u>you think</u> about the city at night you've described.

Summing up — is that doing maths in a lift...

Descriptions are <u>annoying</u> because they <u>aren't</u> always <u>proper questions</u>. Just <u>sum up</u> what <u>you think</u>.

SECTION TEN — ENDING YOUR WRITING

Ending Stories

ENDING STORIES WITH A SURPRISE

Let's face it, stories are a lot more fun than essays.
Unfortunately they're a lot easier to get wrong as well.

Leave Yourself Enough Time For The Ending

The hardest thing about stories is planning them. Sometimes, you work out what you want to write but then you realise you don't have enough time.

> Write a story about a time when you wish you had acted differently.

1) If you find you're running out of time, try to think up a quick ending. Don't put a stupid ending like "Then I woke up. It was all a dream".

2) Just put what happened in the end.

> It was too late. I realised I had spent it all.
> I tried to keep it a secret but my parents found out eventually, and I ended up in lots of trouble. Even now I still feel guilty. My parents still don't trust me with money. I wish I hadn't taken that cash.

That daughter of ours would steal anything!

3) Then put something in at the very end about how it makes you feel now. Make sure it's relevant to the question.

Ending Stories With A Surprise

A really dramatic way to end a story is with a surprise.

> I knew I should never have stolen the vase, so I took it to the cliff and threw it over, watching it smash on the rocks below. I thought that would be the end of it. My guilty secret was gone forever.
> Late that night, the wind was howling around my tent, and the rain was pouring down. There was a huge crash of thunder and a bright flash of lightning. Terrified, I ran out of the tent. There, sitting on top of a tree stump, was the missing vase. It was completely whole. Beside it was the strange old man. His expression had changed. Now he seemed to be smiling.

This is a very exciting ending, because everything is left unexplained.

My story's about glue — I'm sticking to it...

You won't have to write many stories for GCSE English, but you still need to know what to do. Always keep in mind that a good story has to be every bit as well-planned and organised as a good essay. Don't just write any old rubbish. Make sure you leave enough time for a decent ending.

SECTION TEN — ENDING YOUR WRITING

Revision Summary

It's easy to end your writing — you just put your pen down. The trouble is, that won't get you many marks. It's much harder to write a good ending — unless of course you know a few handy tricks. A big part of it is just learning a few simple rules. Go through the questions below to make sure it's all sunk in. After a couple of goes you should be able to answer them all. Then you'll just need a bit of practice, to make sure you can apply the rules. If you're not convinced, consider this — even if you write a bad essay, you can pick up lots of marks if you write a clear beginning and ending. Now that has to be worth learning about...

1) What are the two rules for writing a good ending to an essay?
2) Why should you repeat the words of the question in your ending?
3) How long should you need for each essay in an exam?
4) How long should you leave yourself for ending an essay?
5) What should you do if you're running out of time?
6) What should you do if you've run out of things to write?
7) What should you do if you're still not sure about the answer?
8) Why should you use the exact question words when you're not sure of the answer?
9) What should you do if you've changed your mind about the answer?
10) What three things do you need to remember about ending a letter to friends or family?
11) What do you need to remember about the word limit when you're writing a letter?
12) What do you need to remember about ending a formal letter if you know the person's name?
13) When do you use "Dear Sir/Madam" at the beginning of a letter?
14) Explain the difference between "Yours sincerely" and "Yours faithfully".
15) When you're writing an article, what should the ending cause the reader to do?
16) How should you start your conclusion when you're writing a report?
17) What should you write at the very end of a report's conclusion?
18) When you're writing a description based on extracts, what should you put in the final paragraph?
19) What should you give at the end of a description when there's no real question?
20) What should you do to finish a story if you're running out of time?
21) Why does a surprise make a good ending to a story?

SECTION TEN — ENDING YOUR WRITING

SECTION ELEVEN — COMPREHENSION

Comprehension Questions
Understanding The Questions

Comprehension exercises are about reading short bits of writing and answering questions on them. You're bound to get one of these in your English exam — read this.

You Have To Do Comprehension Without Preparing

In comprehension questions, you don't get to read the the bits of writing until the actual exam. Sometimes you'll be told what the topic will be in advance — and you'll get practice pieces.

The Main Thing Is To Read The Whole Paper Through

1) The first thing to do is read the instructions.
2) Then read the bits of writing until you've got them clear in your mind.
3) You could be asked about media articles, leaflets, travel writing, writing from other cultures and traditions, travel writing or biography.
4) Always read the questions before you answer them. Remember — you need to answer every single bit.
5) Don't waste time — look at the number of marks you can get for each question. If a question is only worth a few marks, don't spend ages on it.

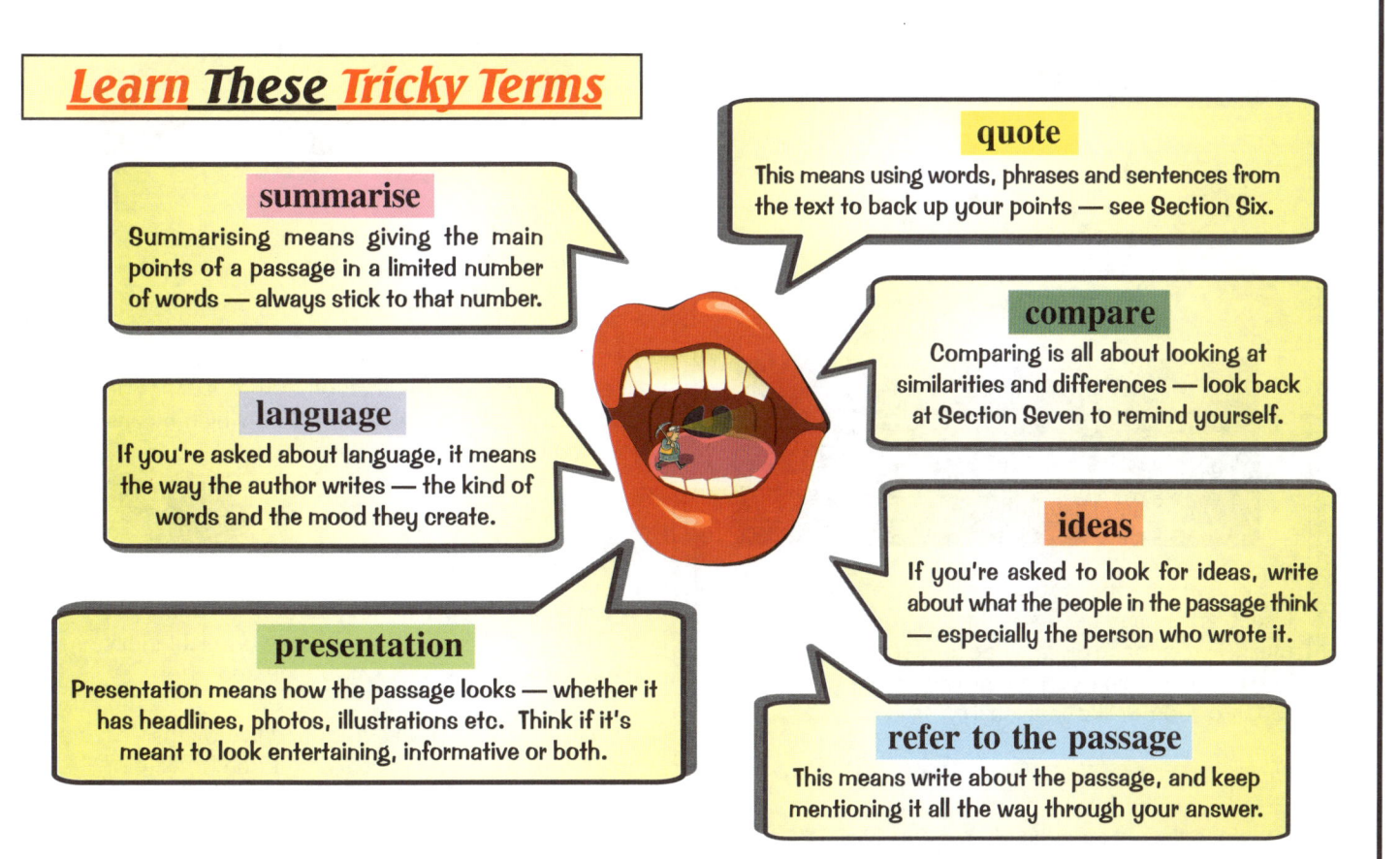

Learn These Tricky Terms

summarise
Summarising means giving the main points of a passage in a limited number of words — always stick to that number.

language
If you're asked about language, it means the way the author writes — the kind of words and the mood they create.

presentation
Presentation means how the passage looks — whether it has headlines, photos, illustrations etc. Think if it's meant to look entertaining, informative or both.

quote
This means using words, phrases and sentences from the text to back up your points — see Section Six.

compare
Comparing is all about looking at similarities and differences — look back at Section Seven to remind yourself.

ideas
If you're asked to look for ideas, write about what the people in the passage think — especially the person who wrote it.

refer to the passage
This means write about the passage, and keep mentioning it all the way through your answer.

Summarise — hidden by sunglasses...

The problem with examiners is they don't put things clearly. That's why you need to know exactly what all these words mean before you turn the page — especially that scary word "comprehension".

Media Texts

NON-FICTION COMPREHENSION

The secret of comprehension is showing the examiners you've understood the passages. Keep that in mind and have a look at the media passages and questions on the next few pages.

Don't Rush Into The Question — Read The Instructions

This tells you that you've got to read all these items before you start the questions. Just do exactly what it says.

Section A: Reading
- Read Item 1, *Insects For Health*, Item 2, *Butterflies in my Stomach*, and Item 3, the newspaper article.
- Answer **all parts** of the question that follows.
- Spend about one hour on this Section.

Here's how long you have to complete this section of the exam. But don't forget — you should spend the first ten minutes reading.

Item 1

INSECTS FOR HEALTH

Have you considered the health benefits of eating insects?

Insects are a tasty and highly nutritious alternative to meat and fish.

Insects:
- are low in all fats
- are high in protein
- contain all the minerals found in other meats
- retain vitamins through the cooking process

A cultivated food source
Insect farms have been scientifically developed to offer a hygienic and disease-free food source. The latest insect-farming methods provide a safe supply of food, unlike traditional livestock.

Farmed insects are fed an exclusively vegetarian diet. Every care is taken to ensure that they eat only nutritious flavour-imparting herbs and grasses.

Cooking with insects

Insects can be used to replace meat in all your favourite meals. Try caterpillar chilli, grasshopper curry, or moth lasagne.

Remember that insects are naturally more tender, so need less time to cook than other meats. They are particularly tasty dry fried or grilled, which means you can use less fat overall in your cooking.

Insects now come ready to cook

You will find insects in the freezer department of all major supermarkets. They are now available fully prepared for cooking, to save time and effort.

Insects are also available fresh and live by mail order. For a list of suppliers and a free booklet of recipes contact the address below.

Insect Marketing Board
PO Box 181
Gloucester
GL3 5XX

SECTION ELEVEN — COMPREHENSION

Media Texts

Non-Fiction Comprehension

Item 2

There's a lot to read in this article so take it slowly — you'll get more marks if you can show you really understand it.

BUTTERFLIES IN MY STOMACH

Marianne Hobgood explains the mission behind her pioneering restaurant SWARM.

The world of food is changing. People are eating things now that their parents would never have dreamed about. A lot of that is due to the SWARM Revolution.

SWARM is the biggest thing in the restaurant trade since the invention of the fork. Last Christmas SWARM-NY was voted one of the New York's top 100 restaurants in a citywide poll. Why? Because it serves the tastiest, healthiest meat in the world — insects.

Before you drop this article in disgust, think about it. Let me put forward the case for insect meat. In the space of one year, New Yorkers went from disgust to delight. Now it's London's turn.

I don't deny that eating your first insect can be a bit of a challenge. Mine was a succulent termite grub, roasted over an open fire in the Australian bush. It was a real struggle to put the thing in my mouth, but once I'd bitten the bullet, so to speak, I knew I was hooked. The flavour was unlike that of any meat I'd eaten before; it was somehow more direct, with more layers and textures.

I quickly got into cooking insects too. They're the most diverse group of animals on earth, and have a correspondingly diverse range of flavours. The intensity of their flavour really enhances the vegetables and fruits they are cooked with. Locusts and zucchini, caterpillars and sea kale, grubs and asparagus, and grilled moths with aubergine are some of the most successful combinations.

If you've never tried them, then you can only take my word for it that insects are tasty. But flavour is not the only reason to choose one food over another.

Health is another concern. Insects are indisputably lower in fat than any other animal product. They are also more wholesome than many other foods we eat. Like crabs, lobsters and prawns they are arthropods, but while lobsters and crabs are scavengers, the insects I recommend you to eat are vegetarians. That has to be healthier.

As the millions who buy organic foods prove, there are also ethical reasons for eating the foods we do. The environmental benefits of insect farming could become extremely important. No other animal can produce such quantities of protein from so little land. Diversifying our eating habits would also add to the overall biodiversity of the planet.

If you're still not convinced, come along and try them. You never know, you might just be bitten by the bug!

SWARM is at
32 Elizabeth Street, London W1
Nearest tube: Bond St

This is a favourite dish at SWARM-NY. If you have a cabbage patch, you will have caterpillars of the large cabbage white butterfly in your garden. Get cooking, I know you'll love it.

Caterpillar Linguine*
serves 4
1 tbsp. olive oil
15-20 large caterpillars
1 clove garlic crushed
1 red onion finely chopped
1 tsp crushed chillies
1 handful chopped parsley
8 tomatoes skinned, deseeded, and finely chopped
400g linguine (uncooked weight)

1. Fry the caterpillars in the olive oil at a high heat until they are just beginning to brown.
2. Reduce the heat and add the garlic, onion, chilli and parsley.
3. When the onion is soft, add the chopped tomatoes and stir.
4. Start cooking the pasta.
5. As soon as the pasta is done drain it, rinse with hot water, and stir into the sauce.
6. Serve with green salad.

45

*Don't try this recipe at home, unless you really know what you're doing!

Section Eleven — Comprehension

Non-Fiction Comprehension — Media Texts

Nearly there now — one more passage to read. Strange stuff, isn't it...

Item 3

Farmers find insect craze difficult to swallow

Ed Lewis

Farmers and landowners staged a rally at Westminster yesterday, protesting at the current craze for eating insects. They claim that the practice devalues their occupation, damages their property and destroys their livelihoods.

Insect consumption has become increasingly popular in recent months. All major supermarket chains now offer live and frozen insects at their larger stores, and many fast food outlets are serving insect alternatives to ordinary meat products.

A statement issued by the National Farmers' Union suggests that the insect eaters are responsible for a 17% fall in sales of conventional meats through domestic channels since June. The statement also goes on to say that the financial implications for many British farmers, who are already struggling to stay in business, will be dire unless the government takes prompt action. The NFU document draws particular attention to what they call an 'invasion' of insect collectors into the countryside.

Ironically, the insect-eaters, many of whom justify their eating behaviour on environmental grounds, are targeting organic farms on their collecting sprees. The use of natural pest controls to avoid excessive damage to the environment, means that insects thrive on organic farms. It is estimated that over £700,000 worth of damage has already been caused by collectors.

The NFU is now calling for insect collection to be properly regulated in partnership with farmers.

Phew — that's the last of the passages. Now here's a typical question.

(a) Read Item 1, *Insects For Health*.
Using the information in the leaflet, explain in your own words the advantages of eating insect meat. *(6)*

(b) Read Item 2, *Butterflies in my Stomach*.
Write down what you think are the writer's **three** most important points in favour of eating insects.
Say whether or not you find them convincing, and explain why. *(6)*

(c) Read Item 3, the newspaper article, and look again at Item 2, *Butterflies in my Stomach*.
What differences do you find between the two articles?
You should write about:
- how the material is presented
- the language used
- the ideas they contain. *(18)*

Split your 50 minutes of writing time between the parts of the question now so you know how long to spend on each one.

- 10 minutes for part (a)
- 10 minutes for part (b)
- 30 minutes for part (c)

Section Eleven — Comprehension

Media Texts

NON-FICTION COMPREHENSION

Here's the hard bit — <u>answering</u> the question. Just <u>read</u> it through and do <u>exactly</u> what it asks.

Sometimes You Need To Explain Things In Your Own Words

1) You've got to use the leaflet here — <u>nothing else</u>. <u>Don't</u> make things up.

2) Watch it — you'll <u>lose marks</u> if you <u>copy</u> sentences straight out of the leaflet.

> **(a) Read Item 1, *Insects For Health*.**
> Using the information in the leaflet, explain in your own words the advantages of eating insect meat. (6)

3) You can pick up <u>six marks</u> here. That means you need to write about <u>six advantages</u> of eating insects to get them all.

4) <u>Read through</u> the passage <u>again</u> and <u>jot down</u> any advantages you find. There are <u>two</u> advantages mentioned in this part — one <u>here</u>... ... and one <u>here</u>.

> Remember that insects are naturally more tender, so <u>need less time to cook</u> than other meats. They are particularly tasty dry fried or grilled, which means <u>you can use less fat</u> overall in your cooking.

Doesn't bother me, I'm not an insect!

Come 'n' have a go if you think you're 'ard enough!

5) Here's <u>part</u> of your answer. Remember to put the points in <u>your own words</u>.

> *Cooking insects is quicker than cooking other kinds of meat because they are more tender. Cooking insects is also healthier, because you can cook them without using as much fat as you would for other meats.*

Some Questions Ask For Your Opinion Of The Passage

First you need to find the <u>three most important points</u>. It's like finding the advantages in part a).

> **(b) Read Item 2, *Butterflies in my Stomach*.**
> Write down what you think are the writer's **three** most important points in favour of eating insects.
> Say whether or not you find them convincing, and explain why. (6)

This part's <u>different</u> — you've got to say what <u>you think</u> about those three points.
Ask yourself if you <u>really believe</u> them... and whether they've <u>convinced you</u> to try <u>eating insects</u>.

Start with what you think is the <u>main point</u>... ...<u>then</u> you need to say <u>why</u> it's a <u>convincing</u> point or why it's not.

> *The writer's <u>most convincing reason</u> for eating insects is that they are tasty. She makes us believe her <u>because</u> she writes in detail about <u>her own experience</u> of eating insects, describing the real taste.*

Don't forget to <u>back up</u> your answer using <u>examples</u> from the passage.

SECTION ELEVEN — COMPREHENSION

Non-Fiction Comprehension — Media Texts

That's <u>two</u> parts of the question down — but this is the <u>trickiest</u> bit.

This Question Is A Short Comparison Essay

> (c) Read Item 3, the newspaper article, and look again at Item 2, *Butterflies in my Stomach*.
> What differences do you find between the two articles?
> You should write about:
> - how the material is presented
> - the language used
> - the ideas they contain.
>
> (18)

These are the things you've <u>got</u> to write about in your answer.

You can pick up <u>eighteen valuable marks</u> for this question — make sure you give plenty of <u>examples</u>.

You Must Answer All The Points In The Question

1) You need to write about <u>how</u> the material is <u>presented</u> in the articles — the <u>big differences</u> between them.

> c) 'Butterflies in my Stomach' has more instant appeal than the newspaper article, mainly because it is in full colour, while the newspaper piece is in black and white...

You don't get me that easily.

2) This is a really <u>obvious</u> point — but remember, as long as it's <u>relevant</u>, you'll <u>pick up marks</u> for it.

3) Then you have to <u>compare</u> the <u>language</u> in the two pieces.

> 'Butterflies in my Stomach' uses cheerful, informal phrases like "bitten by the bug". The newspaper article is more formal and serious. It uses phrases like "devalues their occupation" and "financial implications", which are much more technical and impressive...

4) You've got to <u>back up</u> every point with <u>quotations</u> from the articles.

5) Finally you'll have to write about the <u>ideas</u> in the two articles (with examples, of course).

> Marianne Hobgood claims that eating insects is good for the environment: "No other animal can produce such quantities of protein from so little land". The farmers in the newspaper report say...

Insect spies — they're always bugging me...

<u>Always</u> give <u>examples</u> — it's the <u>key</u> to <u>doing well</u>. Look back at <u>Section Seven</u> for more on <u>comparing</u>.

Other Cultures & Traditions

PRACTICE QUESTION

Here's a kind of comprehension exercise the examiners love — texts from other cultures. They can be stories, essays or poems, and they were often written in different countries.

Answer These Questions Using The Same Method

The main ideas or events might seem a little strange at first, but don't let that worry you.

These exercises are all about how well you've understood the passage, the same as any other comprehension questions.

Section A: Texts from Other Cultures and Traditions

This task will be marked for reading.
The passage below was written by Madame Calderón de la Barca. It describes an episode in her travels through Mexico in the nineteenth century. Read the passage carefully.

From *Life In Mexico*, Letter 33

This is a bit of background information to help you understand what's going on.

It was four o'clock when we left Micatlán, and we travelled quickly until it became almost completely dark. It was our intention to return to our general quarters in Atlacomulco that night. We had a long journey ahead of us, especially because it had been decided there was no way we would try to cross the ravines again at night, since they were considered far too dangerous. Furthermore, an eclipse of the moon was expected, and, in fact, while we were crossing an open field, the moon appeared on the horizon, half in shadow, a rare and beautiful sight.

After a few hours of riding, we suddenly realised that we had lost our way, and worse still, had no way of finding it again. Night had fallen and there was not a single hut in sight; only great plains and mountains and the lowing of distant bulls all around us. We continued on ahead, trusting in luck, though it was difficult to say where she had brought us. By good fortune, our advance riders ran into two Indians, a man and a boy, who agreed to guide us to their village and no further.

After an interminable and exhausting road, which we travelled at a brisk trot, the barking of several dogs announced an Indian village. In the dying light, we could just make out the cane huts, firmly situated between the banana trees, with fenced gardens in front of each one. Our convoy stopped in front of one particular hut, a kind of inn or shop for alcohol, where a naked goblin-like figure, the ideal husband for a witch, was serving cheap brandy to the Indians, most of whom were already drunk.

We dismounted and threw ourselves to the ground, too tired to even think. Someone found us, God knows how, a cup of dreadful hot chocolate. We began to realise that we were completely lost, and so it was agreed to give up our attempt to reach Atlacomulco that night. Instead, we should head for the village of "El Puente", where our guides knew a Spanish family, made up of several unmarried brothers, who, without any doubt, would be delighted to offer us a safe refuge for the rest of the night. We remounted and began our journey, a little restored after the pause in our journey and the dreadful hot chocolate.

Madame Calderón de la Barca

The passage in the exam could be longer or shorter. Either way spend at least ten minutes reading.

SECTION ELEVEN — COMPREHENSION

| PRACTICE QUESTION | # Other Cultures & Traditions |

Nearly finished with this section — make sure you concentrate for these last two pages.

This Question Is About The Way The Piece Is Written

You need to pick out all the mysterious things in the story, then explain why they feel mysterious.

> How does the author create a mysterious mood when she is describing the journey and the Indian village?
>
> **Support your answer by referring to and quoting from the story.**
> *(16 marks)*

There are two things you have to look at here — the journey and the village.

Don't ignore these bits. You've got to give evidence for everything you say or you'll lose marks.

Sometimes the exam paper may give you extra information about the question. If it does, use it to help you plan your answer.

Read Through The Passage Again

1) See if you can work out where the part about the journey ends and the village section begins.

> By good fortune, our advance riders ran into two Indians, a man and a boy, who agreed to guide us to their village and no further.
> -
> After an interminable and exhausting road, which we travelled at a brisk trot, the barking of several dogs announced an Indian village.

2) Now you can look at each part separately to find the ways the author makes them mysterious.

3) Read each part of the passage again and mark everything which feels mysterious to you.

> Night had fallen and there was not a single hut in sight; only great plains and mountains and the lowing of distant bulls all around us. We continued on ahead, trusting in luck, though it was difficult to say where she had brought us.

4) You'll need to use some of the phrases you've underlined to back up your answer.

Cow traditions — that's an udder culture...

All together now — you've got to read the question through. I know I've said it before, but it could save you lots of marks in the exam. It's easy to rush into your answers — and easy to make a mess of them. The question tells you everything you need to do. You just have to get on with it.

SECTION ELEVEN — COMPREHENSION

Other Cultures & Traditions

PRACTICE QUESTION

In _this type_ of question you've got to look at the author's _style_ as well as the facts.

Write About The _Events_ And The _Language Used_

1) _Start_ by getting straight to the _point_ — talk about mystery _straight away_.

> _Everything seems strange in this passage._ The author describes what happens in lots of dramatic detail. That makes her description very mysterious...

2) Now you need to _back up_ your answer with some _examples_.

> The passage starts with the party beginning their journey and the night closing in. Straightaway, there is a feeling of danger and mystery. The author tells us that the ravines were "_too dangerous_" to cross at night, and that "_an eclipse of the moon was expected_"...

3) _Don't forget_ — you've got to _explain why_ your examples are _relevant_... why they _back up_ your point.

> ...This makes the journey seem exotic and magical — the author describes seeing the moon "half in shadow" as the party crossed a field.

4) Your answer needs to show _how_ the mood is created — you have to say _which bits_ make it mysterious and _why_.

> The landscape in which the travellers find themselves lost is eerily empty. There are no people, "not a single hut", only cattle, and even those are "distant".

5) You _must_ write about the _village_ as well — and _give examples_.

> When the travellers arrive at the village, you expect the atmosphere to change. Instead, it remains mysterious. Everything is described as if it happened in a dream. The huts are barely visible in the "dying light", and the person serving drinks at the inn is described as a "naked goblin-like figure, the ideal husband for a witch". It is as if the travellers have arrived in some strange nightmare after their long journey.

Strange men — they can be a bit mister-ious...

Examples and _explaining them_ — that's what comprehension questions are all about.

SECTION ELEVEN — COMPREHENSION

Revision Summary

Hey, it's almost the end of the book — but don't close it just yet. Go through the questions below and make sure you can answer them. After all, comprehension's a pretty important skill — the trick is to prove to the examiners that you've understood what you've read. There are just a few points to remember: You've got to include everything the question asks for in your answer, and you've got to back up what you write with examples from the text. And always check how many marks there are for the question. You should make at least one point or give one example for each mark, or you'll just be throwing them away...

1) What are comprehension exercises about?
2) What's the main thing you need to do to answer comprehension questions?
3) What kind of passages could you be asked about?
4) Why should you look at the number of marks for each question?
5) What does summarise mean?
6) What do you need to write about if you're asked about the language?
7) What does presentation mean?
8) What's the secret of comprehension?
9) Why do you need to look at the amount of time you have for the Section?
10) Why do you need to divide up your writing time?
11) Give two kinds of question you might be asked about a group of passages.
12) What mustn't you do if the question asks you to put things in your own words?
13) What do you need to ask yourself if you have to give an opinion about a point?
14) What must you always give to back up your answers?
15) Why should you always make a point, even if it is really obvious?
16) How should you support your answer to a question on the way a piece is written?
17) What should you do if an exam paper gives you extra information about a question?
18) What do you have to explain about your examples?

SECTION ELEVEN — COMPREHENSION

Index

A

abbreviations 45
accurate quotation 33
add new ideas 24
advantages and disadvantages 37, 85
agree 78
American Dream 28
answering the question 85
answers 12, 19, 34, 37, 42, 80
any old rubbish 42
appearance 16
argument 12, 21, 23, 24, 32, 41, 42, 80
article 25, 36, 37
atmosphere 16, 17, 18
attention span 85
audience 12, 16
Australian bush 91
author questions 17

B

background information 57, 95
backing up your argument 42, 51, 58, 93, 97
balanced argument 47, 49
believe 75, 77, 93
best possible answer 76
big problem 39
biography 89
blood 44
book 59
boring 39, 69, 70, 73
brainwave 24
butterflies 91

C

carry on 48
case 25
casual language 36
certain 75
changing your argument 48, 83
character 14, 15, 16, 17, 18, 38
chocolate 70
choices 19
clichés 70
clues 17
comparing 1, 2, 6, 18, 30, 61-68, 89
comprehension 58, 89-98
concentrate 96
conclusion 85
contradicting yourself 32, 48
convict 57
convincing 78
coursework 11
criticising 77
crossing out 48

D

dangerous sports 12, 25
decision 16
defining 21
describing 12, 15, 17, 18, 38, 64, 69, 70
detailed instructions 13
details 73
detective story 35
devil 55
differences 1, 2, 6, 18, 31, 61, 63, 64, 66, 67, 87, 94
different ideas 47
disadvantages 84
documentary 59
dodo 70
don't panic 23, 66
double speech marks 55
dramatic 87

E

easy questions 19
effect 16, 18
emotions 30
ending your answers 80-88
essay plans 52
events 15, 17
evidence 22, 23, 24, 42, 51
exact question words 34, 81
exaggeration 76, 78
exam 11
examples 1-9, 18, 21, 34, 41, 42, 51, 58, 64
exciting 69, 87
experiences 26
explaining 38, 41, 44, 47, 65, 73, 93
expressing yourself clearly 12, 13
extracts 38, 86

F

facts 37, 72, 97
Fate 27
fear 63
feelings 18, 26, 64, 56, 72
films 58
final plan 24
final point 80
five essay writing steps 6-9
follow on 35
follow your plan 43
for and against 12, 14, 75
formal language 18, 45, 77, 85, 94
formal letters 36, 84
formal reports 37
Frankenstein 51
freezer 90

G

general 65
get to the point 34
Golden Rule 13, 14
grab attention 34
Great Depression 57

H

hand-bag 56
handy hints 12
help 11, 12, 24
hidden meaning 4
highlight 18
historical background 16, 57, 58
how 72
how and why questions 1, 2
however 46
humorous 18

I

ideal 18
ideas 17, 21, 61, 62, 63, 67, 89
images 4, 8, 17, 29, 62, 63, 65, 70
imagine 69, 75
impersonal 76
important ideas 44
improve your grade 11
informal language 18
informal letters 36, 84
information 37, 63, 93
insects 90-94
instructions 11, 67, 89
itching 22

J

jackpot 51
jargon 70

K

key points 76
key words 17, 44

L

language 4, 8, 18, 62, 67, 89, 94, 97
last chance 81
last paragraph 81
layout 61
leaflets 89
letter 12, 36, 75, 84
linguine 91
links 43, 46, 61, 64
literature essays 1-10, 42
long quotations 46

Index

M

magazine 47
magic threes 78
main point 24, 80
manner 16
meaningless describing words 69
media 58, 89–94
memorable 17
method 30, 62, 66
middle of the action 39
monster 55
mood 4, 16, 96, 97
mysterious 96

N

narrator 63
negative points 45, 47, 77
newsletter 37
newspaper article 90
nice 69
nightmare 48
notes 3, 4, 6, 8, 22, 23, 43, 62
novel essays 27
novels 14, 27, 54
numbered points 46

O

obvious details 4
opening paragraph 35, 41
opening sentence 34
opinions 12, 14, 16, 21, 22, 23, 37, 48, 49, 75, 77, 86, 93
order 21, 22
organic 92
original spelling 53
other cultures and traditions 89, 95–97
outline 21
outrageous statements 49

P

pain 18, 26, 66
Pea Head 10
personal 59, 65, 77, 78
persuading 36, 75–78, 85
pink jumpers 76
places 17
planning 6, 9, 11, 12, 21–32, 41, 64, 63, 66, 87
play questions 28
plays 14, 16, 28, 56
plot 15
poems 14, 18, 29, 56, 62
poetry questions 29
point of view 63, 75, 76
police terms 70
polite 77, 84
politicians 78
posh long words 45
positive 47, 75, 77
possible answers 42
practice pieces 89
presentation 89
purpose 12, 13

Q

qualities 17
quarterback 28
question paper 11, 12
question words 34
questions 1, 2, 5, 8, 11, 19, 78
quoting 51–59, 63, 64, 89, 94, 96

R

reactions 16
read every question 11
reading 90
real-life situation 13
reasons 41
refer to the passage 89
referring 96
relevant quotations 54
reports 36, 37
rhetorical tricks 78
rhyme 17
rhythm 17
right answers 42, 47
rooster 70
rude 49, 77
rules 39
running out of things to write 82
running out of time 82

S

save time 22
school newspaper 12, 48, 85
scribble 21
selling a product 76
setting 17, 29
short ending 82
short quotations 55
significance 72
similarities 1, 2, 6, 17, 18, 31, 61, 63, 64, 66, 86
simple language 45
single speech marks 55
situation 37
skills 17, 69
slang 45, 70
small details 4
soldiers 62
speech marks 55
speeches 16, 78
speed bumps 37
sports terms 70
Spud Boy 10
stage directions 56
stating the obvious 62, 63
statistics 59
stick to the point 49
stop and think 22, 48
story 39
storyteller 17
structure 17
style 15, 16, 17, 37, 85, 97
suggest 21
suggestions 30
sum up 84, 87
summarise 80, 89
supermarket 26, 90, 92
surprise 87
suspense 16
sweeping statements 49

T

technical 94
technical terms 70
television 59
telling a story 72
themes 3-6, 9, 15, 62, 67
therefore 46
think 21, 63
thought-provoking 17
thrilling 73
timing 80, 81, 87
title 54, 56
topic 89
travel writing 89
tricky questions 1, 2, 5
trouble 76
twentieth century 67
typical question 12

U

underline 96
understanding 62, 90, 95

W

war 37
waste your time 11, 19
watch 81
what 72
why 72
why and how questions 1, 2
witches 80
word limit 84
word pictures 70
wording your ending 81
write accurately 12, 13
write in paragraphs 11
writers 14, 78
wrong answer 42

Y

your own words 51